In Memory of
Mary Rose Dallal

A REAL-LIFE STORY

SALLY**RIDE**

LIFE ON A MISSION

by SUE MACY

ALADDIN
New York   London   Toronto   Sydney   New Delhi

ALADDIN

An imprint of Simon & Schuster Children's Publishing Division

1230 Avenue of the Americas, New York, NY 10020

First Aladdin paperback edition March 2016

For information about special discounts for bulk purchases, please contact

Simon & Schuster Special Sales at 1-866-506-1949 or business@simonandschuster.com.

The Simon & Schuster Speakers Bureau can bring authors to your live event.

For more information or to book an event contact the

Simon & Schuster Speakers Bureau at 1-866-248-3049

or visit our website at www.simonspeakers.com.

Book designed by Karina Granda

The text of this book was set in Bembo STD.

Manufactured in the United States of America 0216 OFF

2 4 6 8 10 9 7 5 3 1

The Library of Congress has cataloged the hardcover edition as follows:

Macy, Sue.

Sally Ride: life on a mission / by Sue Macy.

p. cm. — (A real-life story)

Audience: Age 8–12.

Includes bibliographical references and index.

[1. Ride, Sally. 2. Women astronauts—United States—Biography. 3. Astronauts—United
States—Biography. 4. Physicists—United States—Biography—Juvenile literature.] I. Title.

TL789.85.R53M33 2014

629.450092—dc23

[B]

2014016685

ISBN 978-1-4424-8854-0 (hc)

ISBN 978-1-4424-8855-7 (pbk)

ISBN 978-1-4424-8856-4 (eBook)

CONTENTS

I would like to be remembered as someone
who was not afraid to do what she wanted to do,
and as someone who took risks along the way
in order to achieve her goals.

—Sally Ride, 2006

INTRODUCTION
BLAZING A PATH

SALLY RIDE WAS ONE OF THE MOST FAMOUS WOMEN in the world, but she also was an intensely private person. She was so private that when she died of pancreatic cancer on July 23, 2012, few people besides her family and close friends knew she had been ill. And many of the millions who admired her were surprised when the last line of her obituary reported that she was survived by her female partner of twenty-seven years. That was the first time this aspect of her life had been made public.

Although Sally Ride lived much of her life in the glare of the spotlight, she did so on her own terms. She gave hundreds of interviews before and after 1983, when she became the first female US astronaut in space. But many interviewers noted that she hardly embraced the celebrity that came with her achievements. Even her younger sister,

Karen, known as "Bear," admitted that Sally tended to protect her privacy. "She doesn't offer information," Bear told a reporter from *Newsweek* magazine in June 1983. "If you want to know something about Sally, you have to ask her." But the reporter noted, "Clearly, Bear never tried to interview Sally, because asking doesn't always work, either."

Despite her reluctance to tell all, Sally Ride believed that young people—and especially young girls—needed role models if they were to aspire to thrilling careers like hers. So she made it her mission to encourage them. After succeeding as a scientist, an astronaut, and a college professor, she became a spokesperson for science and math, using her fame to spread the word. She inspired future scientists and engineers by writing books; running contests, science festivals, and summer camps; and speaking to thousands of kids in person and online.

Fortunately, in reaching out to others, Sally Ride shared more details of her own story. It's the story of a smart, athletic girl whose parents never forced her to follow a particular path but always supported what she chose to do. Those choices took her to space and back (twice) as she blazed a path into the history books as one of the pioneers of the twentieth century. Welcome to her adventure.

CHAPTER 1
GROWING UP

ON THE DAY THAT SALLY KRISTEN RIDE WAS BORN, one of the most popular magazines in the United States featured a short story titled, "Smart Girls Are Helpless." It was May 26, 1951, less than six years after the end of World War II, and the roles of women had undergone several shifts over the previous decade. During the war, the government had depended on women to keep America strong by taking jobs in factories, at shipyards, and in the newly formed all-female branches of the armed forces. Their contributions were crucial to the war effort. When the war was over in 1945, though, most businesses quickly replaced women workers with men. At the same time, many magazines started advising wives to let their husbands take over as breadwinners if they wanted their marriages to last.

"Smart Girls Are Helpless," which appeared in the

Saturday Evening Post, took the same stance as those magazine articles. It focused on an intelligent, independent farmer named Gail who was successful in everything but attracting a man. She preferred to solve problems herself and consistently ignored the advice offered by her handsome neighbor, Charlie. But when Charlie put his farm up for sale, Gail realized that she wanted him in her life. To keep him nearby, she decided to show Charlie that she needed him. She let his prized bull out of its pen and scrambled up a tree with the bull close behind. Charlie heard her cries of "Help!" and came to her rescue. His manly pride was restored.

Stories about strong men and helpless women abounded in the world that Sally Ride entered that Saturday in 1951. But from the start, she was as independent and headstrong as the fictional farmer Gail. Her father, Dale Ride, once remarked that he and his wife, Joyce, "haven't spoken for Sally since she was two, maybe three." The Rides' approach to raising Sally and her younger sister, Bear, was to let them explore the things that interested them. "Dale and I simply forgot to tell them that there were things they couldn't do," her mother said in 1983. "But I think if it had occurred to us to tell them, we would have refrained."

Sally was born in Los Angeles, California, and grew

up in a large ranch house in the Encino district of the city. It was an upscale area; another Encino resident in the early 1950s was a promising young comedian named Johnny Carson. He would go on to host NBC's late-night TV program, *The Tonight Show Starring Johnny Carson*, for thirty years. Sally's father was a professor of political science at Santa Monica Community College. Her mother was a stay-at-home mom during Sally's childhood. Later she taught English to foreign students and spearheaded a group that helped female prison inmates and their families. Both of Sally's parents also were elders in the Presbyterian Church. As such, they were trained leaders who were deeply involved in the welfare and religious life of their church community.

Sally's father was born in Colorado, and her mother in Minnesota. Her mother was the grandchild of immigrants. Three of Joyce's grandparents came from Norway, and the other came from Russia. Sally's father's side of the family immigrated from England, with some of his ancestors arriving in colonial times, a century before the Revolutionary War. Sally's grandfather on her mother's side, Andy Anderson, owned a movie theater in Minnesota before bringing his family to California and starting a successful chain of movie theaters and bowling alleys. Her other grandfather, Thomas V. Ride, worked in banking, first as a bookkeeper and then as a loan adviser.

By the time she was five years old, Sally had already learned to read, thanks in part to her love of sports. She would regularly race her father for first dibs at their newspaper's sports section, and when she got it, she would commit the day's statistics to memory. But she didn't only read about sports. She also played them. "When kids played baseball or football in the streets, Sally was always the best," said her sister. "When they chose up sides, Sally was always the first to be chosen. She was the only girl who was acceptable to the boys." Perhaps it's not surprising that one of Sally's early career goals was to play baseball for the Los Angeles Dodgers.

Besides the newspaper, Sally read lots of books. Her favorites included the Nancy Drew series, featuring the teenaged amateur sleuth who solved mysteries with the help of her friends. She was also a fan of Ian Fleming's James Bond, the dashing British Secret Service agent who first appeared in 1953, and she read some science fiction. Like many other middle-class kids in the 1950s and 1960s, she gave in to her parents' wishes and took piano lessons, but she wasn't happy about it. As an adult, Sally absolutely refused to play the instrument.

When Sally was nine years old, her father took a year off from his teaching career. The Rides spent this sabbatical year traveling through Europe, with Sally's mom tutoring her daughters all along the way. It was the first of several turning points in Sally's life. She returned home with a greater sense of the world and her place in it. Thanks to her adventures and her mother's teaching skills, she also was half a grade ahead of her classmates.

Back in Encino, Dale Ride set out to steer his older daughter toward a sport that might have fewer violent collisions than the ones she was playing with the neighborhood boys. He suggested tennis, and Sally embraced it with passion. In fact, although her father enjoyed the sport himself, he quickly realized that he was no match for her. He quit playing competitive tennis soon after Sally started.

As an individual sport, tennis requires a combination of athleticism and intelligence. Tennis players need power to hit good shots and stamina to keep going through a long match, but they also need to think fast and anticipate where their opponents will hit the ball. Sally definitely had the physical ability to play the sport. To help develop her mental game, Dale sent his preteen daughter to Alice Marble, one of the most celebrated tennis teachers in California.

During her own tennis career, Alice Marble had risen to the number one ranking in the world. She won the US national women's singles title four times from 1936 to 1940, and the Wimbledon singles title once, in 1939. Marble excelled in doubles as well as singles. She won the US national women's doubles title four times, the Wimbledon women's doubles title twice, the US mixed doubles title four times, and the Wimbledon mixed doubles title three times.

Like Sally, Alice had made a name for herself slamming home runs in neighborhood baseball games prior to taking up tennis. In her case, it was her brother who first handed her a tennis racket. "He said, 'Go out and play,'" she once recalled. "I think he wanted me to stop playing baseball with the boys." Alice brought the same strength she showcased in baseball to the tennis court, hitting a cannonball serve that sizzled across the net. Julius Heldman, a former junior champion himself, once wrote that Alice's tennis game "was the product of her tomboy days of baseball." He added, "She played without restraint, running wide-legged, stretching full out for the wide balls, and walloping serves and overheads."

Although Alice had stood up against the best tennis

players of her era, she almost met her match in Sally Ride. "She had talent, a lot of athletic ability," Alice told the *Los Angeles Times* in 1983. "But she seemed so frustrated with it. She would hit me with the tennis ball. I had to duck like crazy. It wasn't that she mis-hit the ball. She had perfect aim."

California was a hotbed of tennis activity for girls and boys in the 1960s, with a circuit of tournaments for gifted players. One of the products of that system was the legendary champion Billie Jean King, who was also a student of Alice Marble (and yet another former passionate baseball player). Despite her behavior at her tennis lessons, Sally embraced the chance to play in weekend tournaments, especially since that meant missing church. Whatever her motivation, she earned a national ranking by the time she was a teenager.

Sally's tennis success opened doors to new opportunities that would shape her life. Chief among them was the offer of a partial scholarship to the prestigious Westlake School for Girls, a private school in the hills above Los Angeles. Westlake's graduates included the former child movie star Shirley Temple, who would go on to become the US ambassador to both Ghana and Czechoslovakia, and future Oscar-nominated and Emmy Award–winning actress Candice Bergen.

When Sally entered Westlake in her sophomore year of high school, she met Susan Okie, a classmate who would grow up to be both a reporter and a medical doctor. In 1983 Okie wrote a series of articles about Sally for the *Washington Post*, starting with her memories from their Westlake days. "Sally was a fleet-footed fourteen-year-old with keen blue eyes, a self-confident grin, and long, straight hair that perpetually flopped forward over her face," she wrote. "We were academic rivals, both on scholarships, and carpooled together. . . . We felt out of place along the actors' daughters and Bel Air belles. Our friendship was instantaneous."

Sally played on Westlake's tennis team each of her three years at the school. She served as captain her senior year, leading a team that swept every division of the local interscholastic tournament without losing a set. Westlake's headmaster in the late 1960s, Norman Reynolds, remembered Sally as being cool and self-confident. He also recalled an up-close-and-personal lesson on how competitive she could be. The headmaster had coaxed Dale Ride onto the tennis court for a friendly doubles match with

Sally and another young woman. Though admittedly not a great player, Reynolds managed to poach a shot at the net and hit the ball past Sally for a point. Sally's response was one that Alice Marble could have predicted. She slammed the next three shots right between the headmaster's eyes at one hundred miles per hour.

Despite the sting, Reynolds admired Sally's competitive spirit. He noted that Westlake aimed to teach students "how to handle that competitiveness, how to keep it in perspective." And indeed, playing tennis at the school did help Sally develop discipline and leadership skills, as well as athletic ability. But Westlake offered excellent academic opportunities too, and Sally embraced them. There was one teacher in particular who inspired her and had a direct influence on the woman she would become.

CHAPTER 2

CHOOSING SCIENCE

BEFORE SHE ARRIVED AT THE WESTLAKE SCHOOL in the late 1960s, Elizabeth Mommaerts was a professor at the University of California at Los Angeles (UCLA). She had a doctoral degree in human physiology, the study of how the body works. At Westlake, she taught a yearlong course in that subject, but her lessons went far beyond what was in the textbook. "Dr. Mommaerts radiated enthusiasm for the intellectual purity of research and offered a view of human nature that seemed to blend chemistry and poetry," wrote her former student Susan Okie in 1983. As an example, Okie remembered a class about human reproduction in which Mommaerts "delivered a series of almost mystical lectures on love, marriage, work and emotional fulfillment."

Sally took the professor's course during her junior year.

While she found the subject matter interesting, it was her teacher's scientific thinking that captivated her. "She was obviously intelligent, clear thinking and extremely logical," Sally told *Newsweek* in 1983. "I had never seen logic personified before." Mommaerts had done scientific research at UCLA, and she embodied the scientific method, the process that scientists follow in formulating knowledge. The process starts when scientists ask a question and do background research to try and formulate an answer. Then they develop a hypothesis (an educated guess) based on that initial research. They test the hypothesis by performing experiments and gathering data from the experiments. Finally, they analyze that data and draw conclusions based on it.

Actually, Sally had been doing some of those things since she was eight or nine years old. "Math and science were always my favorite subjects in school," she said in 2003. "I was pestering my parents for chemistry sets and telescopes and that sort of thing." Her parents did their best to foster her interests. They introduced Sally to friends who were scientists and even bought her a subscription to *Scientific American*, a popular science magazine written for an educated adult audience. "I was, who knows how old, probably too young to read it," she remembered. Even so, she tried from an early age to solve the magazine's brain teasers.

At Westlake, Sally found teachers who promoted the type of problem solving that she loved. But those teachers also supported their students in other ways. Sally said that Mommaerts and another teacher who taught chemistry, physics, trigonometry, and calculus "gave me a lot of confidence in myself at the time when girls kind of need it. And I needed it. I wasn't sure whether I was good enough to go on in science, and they gave me the confidence to go on into college with a science major." Mommaerts, whose daughter also attended Westlake, did not stop teaching when the school day was over. She invited Sally and other students to dinner parties at her home, where she served French food and told stories of her childhood in Hungary. Sally looked at the professor as a mentor. "She cared very much what Dr. Mommaerts thought of her," Okie said.

When it came time to apply to colleges, however, Sally didn't want to abandon tennis. "I was going to be either a scientist or a tennis pro," she said. But it was 1968, four years before President Richard Nixon would put his signature on a new law called Title IX. The law, meant to "level the playing field" for men and women in many areas, led to a great increase in opportunities for women athletes. That included sports scholarships. In 1968, colleges and universities regularly offered sports scholarships to male athletes, but not a single one offered them to female athletes. Sally could play tennis in college, but her athletic skills wouldn't earn her a free ride.

In the end Sally accepted an offer of admission to Swarthmore, a small college just eleven miles outside of Philadelphia, Pennsylvania. She declared herself a physics major and quickly found success as a tennis player. In the spring of her freshman year, Sally won the Middle States intercollegiate tennis championship with a decisive final match. The win was even reported in the *New York Times*, which stated that, "Miss Ride, a Californian, dominated the match from the outset with deep, forceful hitting." Sally was not seeded in the tournament, meaning she was not ranked as a top player based on her previous results. That made her victory all the more impressive.

Another article about Sally's tennis success, in the *Daily Times* of Delaware County, Pennsylvania, turned out to be prophetic. It stated, "Sally Ride, an eighteen-year-old sophomore at Swarthmore College, may one day be the first woman astronaut but for the moment she is the number one woman college tennis player in the East." Years later Joyce and Dale Ride seemed taken aback when a reporter discovered the article in their collection of clippings about their daughter. Sally had never mentioned a desire to be an astronaut to her parents. Indeed, she usually told people she'd first thought about it when she was finishing graduate school.

Sally's tennis victories at Swarthmore left her hungry for more. After three semesters in Pennsylvania, she left school and returned to the West Coast. "I thought I was quitting college to play tennis," she said in 2003. "And then I realized after a month or so back in California that it wasn't the smartest thing to be doing." She decided to continue her education at Stanford University, a top-notch school near San Francisco that also had an excellent women's tennis team. In fact, another Westlake graduate, Julie Anthony, had won the national collegiate doubles crown for Stanford just a few years before Sally arrived.

Though she played on Stanford's varsity tennis team for a few years, Sally eventually dropped the sport to concentrate on her studies. She joked that she gave up tennis because she "took a long, hard look at my forehand and realized that I was not going to make a fortune with that forehand." But her family had other opinions about why she quit. Sally's sister, Bear, thought she didn't have the killer instinct to become a professional player. Her mother thought it was more basic. "She stopped playing tennis because she couldn't make the ball go just where she wanted it to," her mother told *Newsweek*. "It offended her that the ball wouldn't go just where she wanted."

By leaving the tennis world in the early 1970s, Sally just missed out on a revolution that resulted in more tournaments and higher prize money for female pros. One of the leaders of that revolution was Billie Jean King, who also had taken lessons from Alice Marble. King was seven and a half years older than Sally and had been her idol on the tennis court. She had watched Sally play when she was in college and even urged her to leave school to become a pro. But Sally was destined to make her mark in other ways.

Majoring in physics at Stanford, Sally was waging her own quiet revolution as a woman in a man's world. Female students were a definite minority in the physics department at the time. "I wasn't the only one," she remembered in 2003, "but the numbers were fairly small." Added to that, there were no female physics faculty members. What drove Sally was the fact that she "just loved physics," which is the study of matter and energy and the laws that govern how they interact. "I was going to be a research physicist, probably at a university, to teach and conduct physics research."

Why Physics?

In the closing decades of the twentieth century, a knowledge of physics was becoming increasingly important for people who wanted to understand and explore the world. Discoveries by physicists who studied how electrons and other tiny particles behaved under different conditions led to the invention of television, the computer, and the microwave oven. Nuclear power—and nuclear bombs—were developed after physicists harnessed the energy that resulted when one atom split into two. Space travel became possible when physicists and engineers applied the laws of motion developed by Sir Isaac Newton (1643–1727) to build and operate rockets. Newton's laws describe the relationship between an object and forces acting on it, and how it moves in response to those forces.

Of course, you don't have to know how to build a television set in order to watch one. Nor do you have to know where microwaves fall on the electromagnetic spectrum to make a batch of popcorn in a microwave oven. But students like Sally were inspired by the promise of physics to lead them to new horizons. They wanted to be the ones whose dedicated work pushed the limits of what people understood about the world around them and led the way to the next generation of innovations.

In her junior year, however, Sally found another subject that she loved. "Like most science majors, I'd been taking all science, math, astronomy," she said, "and I needed some 'sanity' courses. So I signed up for a course in Shakespeare." She liked it and kept signing up for more. Reading the work of William Shakespeare (1564–1616) was "kind of like doing puzzles," she would later say. "You had to figure out what he was trying to say and find all the little clues inside the play that you were right." Sally's mother, who had hoped she would study English literature, could take some satisfaction when her daughter graduated from Stanford in 1973 with two degrees. She earned a bachelor of science in physics and a bachelor of arts in English.

While she enjoyed her detour into literature, Sally decided to go to graduate school in physics, rather than English. She was accepted at Stanford and focused on astrophysics, which deals with the physics of the universe. Her specific area of study was how free electrons—negatively charged particles that are not attached to particular atoms—behaved in a magnetic field. It related to the research then being done at Stanford on a new kind of laser that used free electrons. But most of Sally's work was theoretical. She worked with mathematical equations to study streams of free electrons moving at the speed of light.

Sally earned her master's degree in physics in 1975. She was close to finishing the work for her PhD in 1977 when she opened up the *Stanford Daily* student newspaper and saw an ad that changed her life. The ad, placed by the Center for Research on Women at Stanford, said that the National Aeronautics and Space Administration (NASA) was accepting applications for astronauts. In particular, NASA was seeking young scientists to serve as mission specialists who would oversee experiments during flights of the new fleet of reusable space shuttles. "The moment I saw that, I knew that's what I wanted to do," Sally remembered in 2006. "I wanted to apply to the astronaut corps and see whether NASA would take me, and see whether I could have the opportunity to go on that adventure."

For Sally, NASA's announcement brought back memories of earlier times. As a child, Sally had shared the excitement of early space missions with her teachers and fellow students. "I can still remember teachers wheeling those big old black-and-white television sets into the classroom so that we could watch some of the early space launches and splashdowns," she said in 2006. "That made a real impact on me, as I think it did on a lot of kids growing up at the time."

The Space Race

On May 25, 1961, President John F. Kennedy asked a joint session of Congress for the funds necessary to land an American on the moon and return him safely to Earth by the end of the decade. It was the latest move for dominance in the Space Race between the world's two most powerful nations, the United States and the Soviet Union. The rivalry began in October 1957, when the Soviets launched the first artificial satellite, *Sputnik 1*. Since then, it seemed, the United States had been playing catch-up.

In 1958 President Dwight D. Eisenhower established the National Aeronautics and Space Administration (NASA) to oversee the nation's civilian space program. On April 12, 1961, while NASA was training the first crop of astronauts for its one-person Mercury spaceflights, the Soviets launched their first "cosmonaut," Yuri Gagarin, into orbit around the Earth. Three weeks later, on May 5, Mercury astronaut Alan Shepard became the first American in space when he took a fifteen-minute flight aboard the *Freedom 7*. The flight was suborbital; Shepard did not orbit the Earth.

John Glenn became the first American to orbit the Earth nine months later. He circled the globe three times during a four-hour, fifty-five-minute mission on February 20, 1962. Other spaceflights continued for both the Soviets and the Americans, while NASA developed the Apollo program to fulfill President Kennedy's mandate. That finally happened in July 1969, when Neil Armstrong and Edwin "Buzz" Aldrin walked on the moon and returned to Earth during the Apollo 11 mission. They were the first of twelve Americans to take moonwalks. Although the Soviets landed unmanned vehicles on the moon as early as 1959, they never landed humans there. They canceled their unsuccessful lunar landing program in 1970.

With her long-buried interest in space reawakened, Sally became one of more than eight thousand applicants who answered NASA's call. She had a feeling she might do reasonably well in the selection process because she was physically fit, a good student, and just a few months away from earning her physics PhD. She was also a good communicator, thanks to all those English papers she had written. And Sally's sports experience proved she was a team player—at Stanford, she had even played women's rugby. Still, she said in 2006, "I didn't think for a minute that I was going to be selected."

Sally had another characteristic that would have worked against her in earlier years. She was a woman. Fortunately, in 1977 NASA was finally ready to diversify the astronaut corps. They were actively looking for the first American women and minorities to travel into space.

CHAPTER 3

THE RIGHT STUFF

ACCORDING TO CAROLYN HUNTOON, A MEMBER OF NASA's astronaut selection committee starting in 1977, there were a few reasons that NASA invited women to apply for the astronaut corps in the late 1970s. First, she said, it was the beginning of the space shuttle program, which meant "we had a new spacecraft, and it was going to be built so that it . . . could have toilet facilities that could accommodate women." But she admits there were larger issues involved. "At that time in our country," she noted, "people were feeling a little bit bad about the way they had treated women . . . and they said, 'It's a federal job and we're going to open it to all races, sexes, religious backgrounds and ages.'"

In fact, in 1972 Congress had passed an amendment to the Civil Rights Act of 1964 that required government agencies to change their hiring practices. The Equal Employment Opportunity Amendment outlawed discrimination "based on race, color, religion, sex, or national origin." Up to that point, NASA had hired seventy-three astronauts, all of whom were male and seventy-two of whom were white. In this first new astronaut class named by NASA since 1967, the organization's selection process would be guided by the new law.

It's not that the idea of female astronauts hadn't come up before. As early as 1959, there were three separate efforts that put women through some of the same physical tests used to choose the nation's first male astronauts, who were dubbed the Mercury 7. One was primarily a publicity stunt orchestrated by the biweekly magazine *Look*. With NASA's cooperation, *Look* followed a female pilot around as she underwent tests and medical examinations and trained and chatted with the Mercury 7 astronauts. The resulting story graced the cover of the February 2, 1960, issue of the magazine with the headline, "Should a Girl Be First in Space?" The pilot, Betty Skelton, was never actually in the running to become an astronaut. "I knew at the time they were not considering a woman really," she said. Still, she relished the chance to prove her abilities. "I felt it was an opportunity to try to convince them that a woman could do this type of thing and could do it well."

Also in 1959, the air force invited another female pilot, fifty-eight-year-old Ruth Nichols, to take some of the astronaut tests at one of its facilities. Nichols had been flying planes since the days of Amelia Earhart. Indeed, she and Amelia had both competed in the first cross-country air race for women in 1929. Over the years Nichols had set speed and distance flying records and was the first woman—and third pilot overall—to land a plane in all forty-eight states. (Alaska and Hawaii had not yet entered the Union.) Nichols continued to set records in the 1950s, and she approached the astronaut tests with the same competitive spirit. She used skills she had developed as an aviator to successfully complete experiments involving weightlessness, isolation, and a centrifuge that quickly spun her around and around. Her excellent results made her confident. "I put in a very strong urge that women be used in spaceflights," she said. Alas, she noted, "they thought of this with horror, and they said under no circumstances."

Not everyone was against seriously considering women as astronauts. Brigadier General Donald Flickinger of the air force had been a big supporter of the Nichols tests, and he was interested in doing more. He teamed up with William Randolph "Randy" Lovelace, chair of NASA's Life Sciences committee, to form Project WISE (Women in Space Earliest). In September 1959 Flickinger and Lovelace recruited pilot Geraldyn "Jerrie" Cobb as the first woman to be tested in their new program. Cobb, then twenty-eight, was a seasoned aviator who had racked up more than 7,000 hours in the air. By comparison, Mercury 7 astronauts John Glenn and Scott Carpenter had only flown 5,000 hours and 2,900 hours, respectively. Cobb had ferried planes to South America, set altitude records, and been voted the 1959 Pilot of the Year by the National Pilots Association.

Unlike Nichols and Skelton, Cobb underwent three phases of testing that systematically evaluated her ability to meet the unique demands of space travel. Phase one involved the physical exams that Lovelace had developed for NASA's selection of the Mercury 7 astronauts. Phase two required Cobb to answer hundreds of questions used to measure her IQ and psychological factors such as her anxiety level and personality traits. It also included isolation tank testing, meant to recreate conditions astronauts would find in space. That required Cobb to float in a tank of water the same temperature as her body, in a silent room and total darkness, as long as she could stand it. The Mercury 7 astronauts didn't take this intense test. They only had to walk and sit in a dark room for three hours. Cobb floated in the tank for nine hours and forty minutes. Then it was on to phase three, which subjected Cobb to a series of grueling airborne and water challenges.

Cobb performed extremely well on all phases of the testing, leading Lovelace to declare, "We are already in a position to say that certain qualities of the female space pilot are preferable to those of her male colleagues." By that time, Flickinger had left Project WISE and Lovelace was running it on his own. But testing continued. Between January and July 1961, eighteen other women took the phase one tests, with twelve of them passing. Two of those twelve took—and passed—the phase two tests before NASA suddenly told Lovelace to cancel all further testing. "They never really gave us an explanation," said Rhea Hurrle, one of the women who passed phase two. "Instead they told us not to talk about it."

Jerrie Cobb was not willing to give up on her dream of being an astronaut without a fight. Neither was Jane Hart, another of the thirteen women who had passed the phase one tests. Hart happened to be married to a US senator,

Philip Hart of Michigan, and she knew her way around the political arena. She wrote letters to members of the space committees of the House and Senate, urging them to restart the women's testing program. Hart's letters and the impassioned speeches Cobb gave around the country were enough to pique the interest of Representative George P. Miller of California, a member of the House Committee on Science and Astronautics. His committee scheduled a special hearing on astronaut qualifications for July 1962.

Both Cobb and Hart testified before the committee. "We seek, only, a place in our nation's space future without discrimination," Cobb said. "We ask as citizens of this nation to be allowed to participate with seriousness and sincerity in the making of history now, as women have in the past." Hart followed, declaring, "It is inconceivable to me that the world of outer space should be restricted to men only." But then it was George Low's turn to speak. Low, NASA's director of spacecraft and flight missions, reminded the committee about President John F. Kennedy's pledge to put "a man on the moon" by the end of the 1960s. Low said that NASA needed to dedicate all its resources toward that goal, rather than toward sending a woman into space.

He also pointed out that one of the requirements for the Mercury 7 astronauts was that they be jet test pilots. Since only men in the military could be trained as jet test pilots, all women were automatically disqualified from the astronaut corps.

Despite their passion, dedication, and skill, Jerrie Cobb, Jane Hart, and the other members of what came to be called the Mercury 13 never got to go up in space. The House committee did not recommend any changes to the process of selecting astronauts. A few months later, the *New York Times Magazine* ran an essay titled, "Why Not 'Astronauttes' Also?" in which a medical doctor explored the concept of female astronauts. "The failure to include women in the NASA pilot program to date," wrote the doctor, "appears primarily due to the simple fact that this is, by and large, a man's world." No doubt Jerrie Cobb and Jane Hart agreed.

It was left to America's rival in the Space Race, the Soviet Union, to send up the first woman. On June 16, 1963, twenty-six-year-old Valentina Tereshkova was sealed into a Soviet *Vostok* spacecraft in the Kazakhstan desert and launched skyward. Tereshkova, a factory worker, was one of five women who had been selected from four hundred applicants to become the Soviets' first female cosmonauts (astronauts). She was not a pilot like Jerrie Cobb and the rest of the Mercury 13. She didn't need to be. The *Vostok* spacecraft was fully automatic and could be manipulated by the crew on the ground. Tereshkova kept a flight log, monitored her health, and took photographs during the three-day mission, orbiting the Earth forty-eight times. It would be her only spaceflight, and indeed, the only Soviet space mission with a woman until 1982.

Back in the United States, NASA's agenda was slowly starting to change after a series of successful moon landings starting in 1969. On January 3, 1972, President Richard Nixon held a press conference to announce his support for a new space shuttle program, whose flights would include a strong component of scientific research. At the press conference, NASA Administrator James Fletcher explained that "no special flight training would be required for passengers, making it possible to send scientists, doctors, artists, photographers—both men and women—into space." It was left to George Low, now Fletcher's deputy administrator, to make sure NASA attracted applications from women and minorities for the project. In a sign of the changing times, he embraced the challenge. After reviewing a draft of the new Astronaut Selection Program, Low wrote to an associate, "I am sure that you are aware of the importance to NASA that every opportunity be presented to these potential candidates [minorities and women] to encourage application, and if qualified selection."

NASA even enlisted the woman who played one of television's most famous space travelers to help them recruit new astronauts. From 1966 to 1969, actress Nichelle Nichols (no relation to Ruth Nichols) starred as communications officer Lieutenant Nyota Uhura in the TV series *Star Trek*. It was a breakthrough part, the first time an African-American actress had an ongoing role as a character on a major TV show who was not a domestic worker. In real life Nichols was dedicated to encouraging women and minorities to pursue careers in science and technology. On NASA's behalf, she toured the country, giving speeches and inviting members of those groups to consider applying for the astronaut corps.

Nichols's efforts, along with ads like the one Sally Ride saw in the Stanford paper, prompted a total of 1,544 women and 6,535 men to fill out the short paper application that NASA sent potential astronauts. Those who made the initial cut received a longer application that asked about their medical histories and their motivation for becoming an astronaut. The selection committee also conducted detailed interviews with any people that the applicants listed as references. They used all this information to choose approximately two hundred finalists. Those finalists were brought to Johnson Space Center (JSC) in Houston, Texas, in groups of twenty for a week of interviews, tests, and introductory briefings. Sally's group ventured there in October 1977. "Nobody knew what to expect," Sally told *Ms.* magazine in 1983. "From what we'd heard and read, we thought they'd put us in centrifuges, dunk us in ice water, hang us up by the toes—anything!"

NASA Locations

As an agency of the federal government, NASA makes its headquarters in Washington DC. There, under the leadership of its chief officer, called the administrator, it oversees the work of scientists, engineers, managers, and other personnel at ten field centers and additional test facilities across the country.

One of NASA's field centers, Lyndon B. Johnson Space Center (JSC) in Houston, Texas, is home to the

NASA astronaut corps and became the lead center for space shuttle activities. JSC is also home to Mission Control Center, which directed all space shuttle missions. Another field center, John F. Kennedy Space Center (KSC) in central Florida, served as the launch site for all space shuttle missions and the landing site for most of them.

There were lots of tests to determine how the finalists would respond to the physical and psychological challenges of being an astronaut, but none involved being hung by their toes. Instead, each candidate took a thorough medical exam. It included a stress test that measured heart performance during exercise, an electroencephalogram (EEG) that measured brain activity, and hearing and vision tests, among others. Candidates also were examined by two psychiatrists. "The first guy was what I would have expected," said Sally. "He was very warm. 'Tell me about yourself. Do you love your mother? Why do you love her? How does your sister feel about you?'" The second one was more abrupt. He "was sort of the bad-guy psychiatrist, who tried to rattle you," Sally said.

NASA required astronauts to be sixty to seventy-two inches tall, have normal hearing and blood pressure and twenty-twenty vision (with glasses or contact lenses), and have no history of serious illnesses. There was no age limit. Beyond that, the selection committee looked at the results of the candidate's psychiatric exams and at recommendations written by his or her scientist colleagues. Another important factor was the candidate's answers to questions posed in an hour-long interview with the ten members of the committee. George Abbey, director of flight operations and chair of the committee, said they were looking for certain types of people. "Team players," he said. "These people have to have initiative. They have to be self-starters. And they *have* to be team players."

When the week was up, Sally returned to California to work on her PhD degree . . . and to wait. Early in the morning on January 16, 1978, the twenty-six-year-old was awakened by the urgency of a ringing telephone. George Abbey was on the line, and he had good news. He told her, "We've got a job here for you, if you're still interested in taking it." It was a moment before Sally could respond. "I thought maybe I was dreaming," she remembered. "But of course, I was thrilled. My biggest frustration was that it was five or six in the morning in California, so all my friends and family were asleep. I wasn't sure that I should wake them up to give them the news!"

Sally admitted that her mom didn't quite know what to think about her daughter's new job. Her father, on the other hand, was very supportive and very excited. And so was Sally. The greatest adventure of her life was about to begin.

CHAPTER 4

SETTLING IN

GEORGE ABBEY WAS VERY BUSY THE MORNING OF January 16, 1978. In all, he contacted thirty-five men and women to offer them spots in the first class of space shuttle astronauts. Six of the new recruits were women, three were African-American men, and one was a Japanese-American man, giving a welcome diversity to the astronaut corps. All thirty-five would be known as astronaut candidates (AsCans) until they completed their training period. Although these men and women weren't scheduled to report for training until July, their lives started to change almost immediately.

At one p.m. on January 16, NASA officials held a press conference in Washington DC to announce the identities of the thirty-five new AsCans. And in Palo Alto, California, Stanford University held its own press conference to introduce their NASA recruit to the world. It was the first of many times astronaut Sally Ride would meet with reporters, and it made an impression. "I mean, my gosh," she remembered in 2002, "I was a PhD physics student. Press conferences were not a normal part of my day."

Two weeks after the announcement, the thirty-five AsCans gathered at Johnson Space Center for three days of orientation, as well as more rounds with reporters. It was the first time all the female AsCans got to know one another. Besides Sally, they included Kathryn Sullivan, a geologist from California; Judith Resnik, an electrical engineer from Ohio; Shannon Lucid, a biochemist who grew up in Oklahoma; Margaret Rhea Seddon, a surgeon from Tennessee; and Anna Fisher, a chemist and medical doctor who grew up in California. Lucid, the oldest of the women at thirty-five, was the sole female AsCan with children. She had three.

Carolyn Huntoon, the only woman on the astronaut selection committee, served as a mentor to the female candidates. She started by focusing on their dealings with the press. Huntoon told the women that while their work as astronauts was fair game for media analysis, it was up to them how much of their personal lives they wanted to reveal. Would Lucid and Fisher talk about their husbands? Would the others discuss their social lives? What was the best way to avoid answering a question that they judged to be too personal? To make sure they were all on the same page, the women compared notes after every interview. They told one another what questions the interviewer asked and how they answered them.

Not surprisingly, the women and minority men attracted the most attention from reporters. "We eventually came to refer to our class as 'ten interesting people and twenty-five standard white guys,'" Kathryn Sullivan said in 2007. She described her first dizzying media day. "The twenty-five standard white guys were done about 4.3 minutes after the formal event, left, and had the whole rest of the day free. They could go run. They could do whatever they wanted. The other ten of us, we were there till Lord only remembers. I don't remember what time—way late."

After this initial frenzy of activity, the new AsCans returned home to wrap up jobs and projects and family matters before moving to Houston. Sally used those months to finish the work on her PhD thesis, the long research paper she needed to earn her degree. "It was almost perfect timing for me," Sally said. She completed her research and writing and then defended her thesis back at Stanford—answered questions about it in front of a panel of professors. She said, "I literally defended my PhD thesis, got in the car, and drove to Houston."

Meanwhile, Johnson Space Center was getting ready for its new female recruits. The most obvious change involved the astronauts' gym, which had no women's locker room. Mercury 7 astronaut Donald "Deke" Slayton, then director of flight crew operations, was in charge of the project. At first Slayton proposed just putting up a curtain in the men's locker room to give the women a bit of privacy, but he eventually reconsidered. By the time Sally and the others arrived in Houston, a separate women's locker room was waiting for them.

In July 1978 there were about four thousand engineers and scientists working at JSC. Only five or six were female, according to Sally. So the female AsCans doubled the number of women in technical roles at the space center. Carolyn Huntoon reported that some of the men there took a while to get used to the female recruits. She said, for example, that at the beginning of a meeting someone might complain that no astronaut was present, when in fact a female astronaut was in the room. But most of those slights came from the old guard. The men in the Sally's astronaut class were at ease with their female colleagues. "The selection committee was looking for men that were comfortable working with women, that were used to working with women, and that had no problem working with women," Sally said in 2002, "and they succeeded. . . . We really didn't have any issues at all within our group."

Eventually, even the old guard came around. Alan Bean was head of the Astronaut Candidate Operations and Training Group when Sally's class arrived at JSC. In 1969 he had landed the lunar module on the moon during the Apollo 12 mission. And he had all kinds of notions about women's abilities. "Many people around here had in their minds that these would be women doing men's jobs," he told *Texas Monthly* magazine in 1981. "I know I thought that. Astronauts, to me, were men; they had to think about computers and flying—male things. But I've changed that opinion. The job of astronaut is just as female as it is male. Females intuitively understand astronaut skills. They perform the mental and physical tasks as well as males do."

Sally's astronaut class of thirty-five was so big that it was divided into two teams for training purposes. The teams were led by the two oldest members: John Fabian, age thirty-nine when the AsCans reported for duty; and Frederick Hauck, age thirty-seven. The training regimen involved a lot of classroom work. "It was just like being back in college," Sally remembered. "We studied systems and schematics and other things that I was well trained to do." The AsCans attended lectures on engineering and computer science. They took classes in areas of science, such as geology and oceanography, that they would need to know to do experiments in space. They visited different NASA facilities across the country to learn about projects going on at those locations. And they studied the space shuttle inside and out until they were familiar with every detail of this new vehicle.

About the Space Shuttle

NASA designed the space shuttle to take off like a rocket and land like a glider. The shuttle was made up of four main components, including two solid rocket boosters (SRBs), an external fuel tank (ET), and an orbiter vehicle (OV). The solid rocket boosters were cast off after launch. They floated back to Earth attached to parachutes and then were refurbished and used again. The external fuel tank, containing liquid hydrogen and liquid oxygen, separated from the OV just before entering orbit and largely burned up in the atmosphere. (Any fragments that fell to Earth landed in the oceans.) The crew lived in and performed their work in the reusable orbiter vehicle. At the end of a mission, this vehicle fired its engines to drop out of orbit, reenter Earth's atmosphere as a glider, and land on an airport runway.

From 1981 to 2011, NASA would undertake a total of 135 shuttle missions. Five different orbiter vehicles would be used: *Columbia*, *Challenger*, *Discovery*, *Atlantis*, and *Endeavour*. Flights would carry from two to eight crew members. They would also carry cargo, called payloads. Some of the payloads were equipment for scientific experiments that the astronauts would perform. Others were exploratory technology, such as satellites, that the astronauts would launch into orbit. For example, astronauts aboard the space shuttle *Discovery* would launch the Hubble Space Telescope in 1990, and it would be serviced and upgraded during five subsequent shuttle missions. Over the years, the powerful Hubble would take pictures of galaxies that are billions of light-years away from Earth and would lead to major breakthroughs in scientists' understanding of the universe.

Shuttle Fast Facts

- **LENGTH (OV ALONE):** 122 feet (37.2 meters)

- **LENGTH (ET, OV, SRBS):** 184.2 feet (56.1 meters)

- **WINGSPAN (OV):** 78 feet (23.8 meters)

- **WEIGHT AT LIFTOFF (OV, ET, TWO SRBS):** 4,470,000 pounds (2,028 metric tons)

- **LONGEST MISSION:** STS-80, seventeen days, fifteen hours, fifty-three minutes (1996)

Still, not all of the AsCans' training took place on the ground. Soon after arriving in Houston, they were fitted with flight suits and helmets and taken for rides in NASA's Northrop T-38 supersonic jets. These two-seater planes served as jet trainers for the future astronauts, and everyone, including mission specialists like Sally, had to learn to fly them. "The flying was totally foreign to me," said Sally, "and an awful lot of fun. I really enjoyed both the ground school and then the flight training itself." Since the space shuttle would return from its missions to land as a glider, training on T-38s taught the AsCans practical lessons about flying—and landing. They learned to make quick decisions under real-world conditions while blasting through the air at breakneck speeds.

NASA initially planned a two-year training period for the AsCans, but officials eventually decided that was too long. So in August 1979, after thirteen months in Houston, the astronaut candidates became full-fledged astronauts. Their training complete, the thirty-five men and women then took on individual assignments related to the space shuttle, which was still being tested and programmed. Sally was one of the astronauts responsible for helping to develop the shuttle's robot arm, officially called the Shuttle Remote Manipulator System (SRMS or just RMS). She spent a lot of time in Toronto, Canada, where this hinged fifty-foot-long, nine-hundred-pound arm was being built. She and her colleagues worked out checklists for using the arm and procedures to follow if it malfunctioned in space. They also tested the hardware as it was being assembled.

"Until you actually start using something, it's very difficult to make predictions on how well it's going to work," Sally said. The robot arm was designed to move materials such as satellites in and out of the space shuttle's cargo bay.* It was up to the engineers in Canada, along with Sally and other astronauts, to figure out the best way for the humans inside the shuttle to control the arm when it was outside the vehicle. One mistake could damage a costly satellite or even the shuttle itself, endangering lives. Sally and her colleagues had to imagine all the things that could go wrong while using the robot arm. Then they had to write instructions for astronauts on how to prevent those problems or, if worse came to worst, how to recover from them.

---

* Satellites are artificial, computer-controlled objects placed in orbit to help people on Earth with such tasks as monitoring the weather and improving communications and navigation. Satellite TV, Global Positioning System (GPS) receivers, and satellite telephones all depend on information from satellites.

By July 1978, when Sally's class arrived in Houston for their training, the two-man crew for the initial space shuttle mission had been chosen. Commander John Young had first flown into space as the pilot of *Gemini 3*, in 1965, and he also flew on *Gemini 10*, *Apollo 10*, and *Apollo 16*. (Project Gemini involved ten missions in 1965 and 1966, each with two astronauts onboard. Project Apollo flew eleven missions, each with a trio of astronauts, from 1968 through 1972.) During that last trip, John Young walked on the moon. Pilot Bob "Crip" Crippen was still waiting for his first venture into space, but he had been part of the astronaut corps since 1969. As such, he had provided ground support for all three Skylab missions in the 1970s. On those missions, American astronauts flew to the Skylab, the United States' first orbiting space station, and stayed as long as eighty-four days before safely returning to Earth.

Young and Crippen would use their flight aboard the space shuttle *Columbia* to test the systems and components of that complicated craft. All thirty-five of the new astronauts also would take part in the mission, dubbed STS-1 (for "Space Transportation System"). The new astronauts were paired up and assigned to T-38 jets as chase crews.

These crews would fly alongside the space shuttle after it reentered the Earth's atmosphere and prepared to land. They would match the shuttle's speed and altitude and communicate those numbers to Commander Young so he could be sure the readings on the shuttle were accurate. Chase crews also would assess the shuttle for any visible damage to the surface materials that protected it from the extreme heat of reentry. Officials needed to know the condition of the surface before the shuttle landed, since the process of landing could cause additional damage.

Sally was paired with Francis "Dick" Scobee on the STS-1 chase crew, but they missed out on the excitement. They awaited the shuttle at the Kennedy Space Center, in Florida, while other crews were ready to go near the White Sands Space Harbor in New Mexico and Edwards Air Force Base in California. Edwards was the intended landing site, but officials would alter the plans if bad weather made landing there unsafe. In the end, though, the shuttle did land in California.

Young and Crippen lifted off on April 12, 1981. Exactly twenty years before, Yuri Gagarin of the Soviet Union had become the first human being to travel in space. With their flight's successful conclusion on April 14, the era of the

space shuttle had begun. Through the end of the twentieth century and beyond, five reusable shuttles from the
United States would fly astronauts and scientists to space
an average of over four times a year. There would be lots
of triumphs and two awful tragedies, and Sally Ride would
be front and center as much of this history was made.

CHAPTER 5

STEPPING UP

WHEN PLANS FOR THE SPACE SHUTTLE *COLUMBIA'S* second mission got underway, Sally Ride received a new assignment. She would be one of several capsule communicators, or CapComs, for the flight. CapComs are stationed at mission control in Houston during a spaceflight. They are the communications link between the astronauts in space and the personnel on the ground, relaying information back and forth. Since STS-2 was the first flight to carry the RMS (robot arm), officials wanted to be sure they had a CapCom who knew the ins and outs of that technology. All the checklists and procedures Sally had helped to develop for the RMS would come in handy as she aided her two fellow astronauts in space.

Those astronauts, Richard Truly and Joe Engle, also asked Sally to help with their mission in other ways.

"They were both very, very interested in observing Earth while they were in space," said Sally, "but they weren't carrying instruments other than their eyes and their cameras." She worked with Dr. William Muehlberger, a geology professor who advised NASA on how to teach astronauts to distinguish different features from space. "The crew had to learn how to recognize the things that scientists were interested in," said Sally. "Wave patterns on the surface of the ocean, rift valleys, large volcanoes, a variety of different geological features on the ground." Here again, Sally served as a communications link, this time between Truly and Engle and the scientists. She helped the crew know what they were looking at from space so their photographs would give scientists on Earth a new perspective on the exact features they were studying.

Not all of Sally's CapCom responsibilities were quite as serious. It also fell to her to arrange for the recordings that would be used as wake-up calls for the STS-2 astronauts during their three-day mission. These recordings were a bit unusual, as they came from the cast of the "Pigs in Space" science fiction sketches featured on the popular TV series *The Muppet Show*. Ride worked with Muppets personnel to secure two original comedy routines from

Miss Piggy and the rest of the crew of the fictional space-ship *Swinetrek*. On the last morning, the shuttle astro-nauts were also treated to a rendition of the patriotic song "Columbia, the Gem of the Ocean."

Sally served as a CapCom for STS-2, which flew from November 12 to 14, 1981, and STS-3, which was launched on March 22, 1982, and landed on March 30. Her work on both flights was first-rate, and people were starting to notice. Bob Crippen, the pilot of SRS-1, was among her admirers. "I like people that don't get too excited, too emotional, that keep a fairly even keel," he said in 1983. "Those kinds of people work well with me."

As it happened, early in 1982 Crip was named com-mander of the seventh space shuttle flight, STS-7, and he would help to choose the crew. It would be the first shuttle crew made up of members of Sally's astronaut class of 1978. Crip and others thought one of those crew members should be a woman. "I think NASA manage-ment on up the chain just felt that it was time," he said. Crip believed Sally was the right person for the flight for a number of reasons. "She was one of our experts on the Remote Manipulator System, which was critical to what we were doing on this mission," he told an interviewer in 2006. He added, "We just got along well. That's really important when you've got a crew because you've got to work together. I knew that she would integrate well with the other crew members that we had onboard."

On April 19, 1982, shortly before the regular Monday morning Astronaut Office meeting, Sally got a call to report to George Abbey's office. "I have to admit, I sort of knew what it was about," Sally said. Abbey, still director of flight operations, told Sally she'd been assigned to STS-7. Then he brought her up to see Christopher Kraft, the director of the Johnson Space Center. "He reminded me that I would get a lot of press attention and asked if I was ready for that," she said. "His message was just, 'Let us know when you need help. . . .' It was a very reassuring message, coming from the head of the space center."

From there, Sally returned to Abbey's office to wait for two of her STS-7 crew members, Crip and John Fabian. When they arrived, the group telephoned the fourth member, Frederick "Rick" Hauck, who was out of town. (A fifth astronaut, Norman "Norm" Thagard, would be added later to make this the first shuttle to fly with more than four onboard.) That same day, NASA issued a press release naming the astronauts assigned to the seventh, eighth, and ninth space shuttle missions. "Three Shuttle Crews Announced," read the headline. There was no fanfare drawing attention to the fact that the first US woman to venture into space would be aboard STS-7, or that the first African-American space traveler, Guion Bluford Jr., would be aboard STS-8.

To further protect Sally from the glare of publicity, NASA denied all requests for interviews while the astronauts trained for their mission. "They did a really good job shielding me from the media so that I could train with the rest of the crew and not be singled out," said Sally. "We also tried to get across that spaceflight really is a team thing."

Four of the STS-7 astronauts—Sally, John, Rick, and Norm—were members of the class of 1978. And while they were excited about being chosen, they tempered their celebration out of respect for colleagues who still hadn't been assigned to a flight. "Somebody had to be first, and everyone was adult enough to understand that," said Carolyn Huntoon. Still, she couldn't help but notice a somberness among those who weren't chosen. "Everyone is an achiever, and they're used to being first."

Since four of the five members of the shuttle team had never flown in space before, there was a lot to learn.

STS-7 would be the second voyage of a new space shuttle in NASA's growing fleet, *Challenger*. Sally divided much of her time between doing launch and reentry simulations with Crip and Rick and RMS training with John and Norm.* But the whole crew trained together to prepare to launch the two communications satellites they would have onboard. They also spent a lot of time together in the shuttle simulator, the earthbound cockpit that recreated the sights, sounds, and motions of liftoff and landing. "We got to know each other very, very, very well," said Sally. "We never had any issues at all and got to be very, very good friends through the training."

Despite the intensity of training, Sally managed to move forward with her personal life during this time. She had been living with another astronaut from the class of 1978, Steven Hawley, and on July 26, 1982, they quietly got married. Sally piloted a plane to the ceremony, which took place at Steve's parents' home in Kansas. Her wedding attire consisted of jeans and a rugby shirt. It was a small affair, with only the bride's and groom's immediate families in attendance. The couple even kept the officiating

---

* Simulations are computer-based representations of the actual experience, used for training or practice.

in the family. Sally's sister Bear was now a Presbyterian minister. She performed the ceremony with Steve's father, Bernard Hawley, who was a Presbyterian minister as well.

Steve was a redhead, seven months younger than Sally, and as outgoing as she was reserved. Like Sally, he had two majors in college, graduating from the University of Kansas with bachelor's degrees in physics and astronomy. He then earned a PhD in astronomy and astrophysics from the University of California, Santa Cruz. After their marriage, Sally and Steve moved into a house near the Johnson Space Center that they decorated with posters and photographs of T-38 jets, space shuttles, a moon landing, and the logo designed for their astronaut class. They shared a love of sports and TV, and tended to try and stump each other with trivia challenges in both areas. When it came to mealtime, they barbecued, but didn't cook much. "We eat from hand to mouth around here," Sally told her friend, journalist Susan Okie, "and we tend to survive mostly on potato chips."

While Sally was training for STS-7, Steve was named as a crew member on the twelfth shuttle mission, scheduled for launch in 1984. But before that, Sally would take her place in history. The launch of STS-7 was originally planned for April 1983. However, because of problems with the previous shuttle mission, it was rescheduled for June 18. On May 24, NASA finally gave reporters the chance to ask questions of Sally and the rest of the crew at a preflight press conference. The next day, the *Los Angeles Times* noted that the press conference drew several times as many reporters as usual. Not surprisingly, most of the reporters' questions were directed at Sally. "I think that it's too bad that our society isn't further along and that this is such a big deal," she told them. "It's time that people realized that women in this country can do any job they want to do. There still are some people out there who need to be enlightened."

Sally was no doubt referring to some of the reporters in the audience. One, from *Time* magazine, asked her whether she reacted to stressful situations by weeping. Sally's reaction? She looked at her crewmate Rick Hauck and asked, "Why doesn't anybody ask Rick those questions?" Another reporter asked if she planned to wear a bra in space, and she pointed out it wasn't really necessary in zero gravity. When a third reporter asked if she planned to have children, Sally ignored the question altogether. After fielding those and other queries, she looked out at the press and said, "I am so excited to get a chance to fly that I am going to ignore all you people."

For the remaining weeks before launch, Sally was able to disregard most of the hoopla and concentrate on training for the flight. But the media were buzzing with quips and commentaries about her place in history. Sally's old Encino neighbor Johnny Carson, star of *The Tonight Show*, joked that the shuttle launch had been postponed until she could find a purse to match her shoes. Jim Borgman, a political cartoonist for the *Cincinnati Enquirer*, captured the absurdity of reporters' questions by drawing a flabbergasted Sally walking away as interviewers shouted out, "Who will make the coffee on board?" "Will you be tidying up the cabin?" and "What will you do in your free time—knit?"

Meanwhile, columnist Ellen Goodman wrote that Sally was experiencing a classic case of "First Womanitis," the phenomenon of being the first woman to achieve a sought-after goal. "As a First Woman, she is watched and called upon to explain her very existence in a way that her co-travelers are not," Goodman wrote. "She is asked opinions on everything 'female' . . . and everyone offers opinions about her." Goodman noted that First Women carry the frustrations of those who never got the chance to do what she was doing,

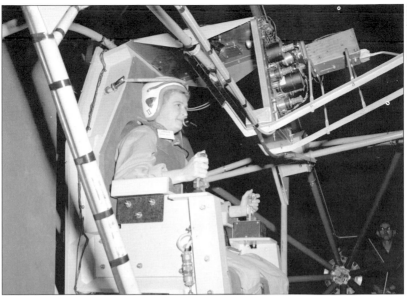

In 1960, Mercury 13 pioneer Jerrie Cobb prepares to undergo tests in NASA's gimbal rig, a cage that simulated the rolls, pitches, and tumbles that scientists expected astronauts to encounter in space.

The first American female astronaut candidates gather at the Johnson Space Center on January 31, 1978. They are, from left to right, Rhea Seddon, Anna L. Fisher, Judith Resnik, Shannon Lucid, Sally Ride, and Kathryn Sullivan.

Sitting in front of a photograph of a space shuttle about to land are the crew members of STS-7. Seated, left to right, are Sally Ride, Robert Crippen, and Frederick Hauck. Standing, left to right, are John Fabian and Norman Thagard.

NASA's official photograph of the crew of STS-41G includes (seated, left to right) Jon McBride, Sally Ride, Kathryn Sullivan, and David Leestma and (standing, left to right) Paul Scully-Power, Robert Crippen, and Marc Garneau.

Just days before her first spaceflight in June 1983, Sally Ride sits in the T-38 Talon jet, which will carry her from the Johnson Space Center in Houston, Texas, to the Kennedy Space Center in Florida.

As part of her astronaut training, Sally Ride learned to fly a Northrop T-38 Talon jet like this one. The T-38 can reach a maximum speed of Mach 1.6, which is faster than the speed of sound.

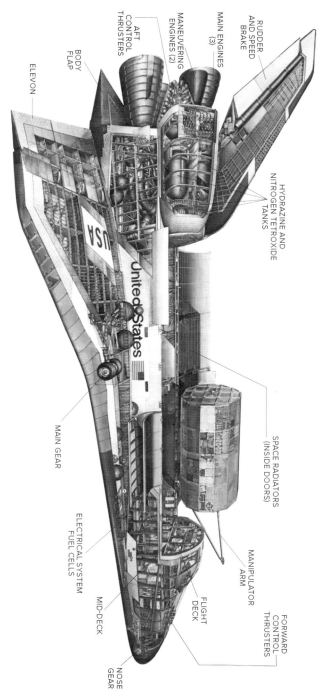

RUDDER
AND SPEED
BRAKE

MANEUVERING
ENGINES (2)

MAIN ENGINES
(3)

AFT
CONTROL
THRUSTERS

BODY
FLAP

ELEVON

HYDRAZINE AND
NITROGEN TETROXIDE
TANKS

SPACE RADIATORS
(INSIDE DOORS)

MAIN GEAR

MANIPULATOR
ARM

FORWARD
CONTROL
THRUSTERS

ELECTRICAL SYSTEM
FUEL CELLS

FLIGHT
DECK

MID-DECK

NOSE
GEAR

Courtesy of NASA

This cutaway diagram highlights many of the parts of the space shuttle. The commander and pilot controlled the mission from the flight deck, while the mid-deck was where the toilet, sleep stations, galley, and other amenities for daily living could be found.

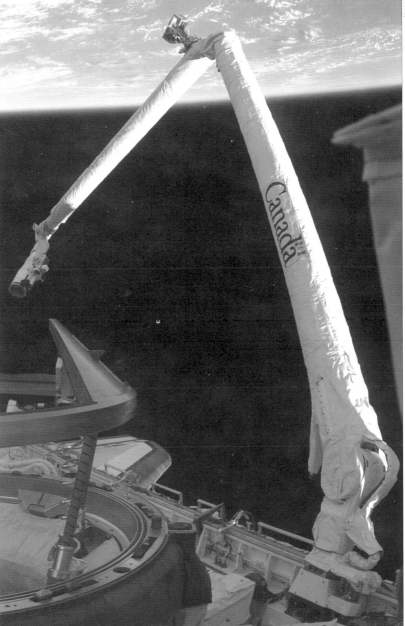

Closeup of the space shuttle's Canadian-built Shuttle Remote Manipulator System (robot arm), which Sally Ride operated on both of her missions.

During her first shuttle mission, Sally Ride communicates with ground controllers from the flight deck of the *Challenger*.

Official mission patch of STS-7. Note that the robot arm is positioned to make a "7." The image in the circle on the right uses the standard symbols for male and female to indicate that the flight carried four men and one woman.

Official mission patch of STS-41G. It includes a Canadian flag next to the name of the Canadian astronaut, Marc Garneau, and a male or female symbol next to the name of each crew member.

Sally Ride jokes with her husband, Steve Hawley, in sunglasses, soon after returning to Houston with the STS-7 crew.

Sally Ride, right, with tennis star Billie Jean King as they are both inducted into the California Hall of Fame in 2006.

Sally Ride's partner, Tam O'Shaughnessy, stands with President Barack Obama in the East Room of the White House on November 20, 2013. Tam was there to accept the Presidential Medal of Freedom—the nation's highest civilian honor—on behalf of Sally.

such as Jerrie Cobb and the Mercury 13. "Being a full-fledged First Woman means taking every step for womankind," wrote Goodman. "It's not easy, but the company is fine."

Years later Sally confirmed that she felt the added pressure of being the first American woman in space. "It came with a lot of responsibility," she said. "I was very aware through the training that I needed to understand my job well enough and perform it well enough in space that I wouldn't cast doubt on whether women should be in the astronaut corps." She agreed that there were similarities to the barrier-breaking achievements of her tennis idol, Billie Jean King. In particular, she cited King's 1973 "Battle of the Sexes" victory over the self-proclaimed "male chauvinist pig," Bobby Riggs. King had said she just couldn't lose to Riggs—a man almost twice her age—because it would impact the public's acceptance of women's tennis. "It's the same kind of thing," said Ride. "I just couldn't make any mistakes."

By the time her alarm clock rang at three fifteen a.m. on June 18, Sally was as ready as she could be. Over the past fourteen months, she had studied every schematic, memorized every fact and figure, and practiced every procedure over and over again. At the astronaut crew quarters, she and her four crewmates put on their identical lightweight, blue, cotton-blend flight suits, ate a light breakfast, and boarded a van for their nine-mile trip to the launch pad. The First Woman was about to carry her sisters into the cosmos.

Breakthroughs in Women's Rights

Sally Ride's journey into space was part of a wave of social change for women in American society. Here are some highlights from the two decades leading up to her flight.

1963: In her influential book, *The Feminine Mystique*, author Betty Friedan attacks the assumption that a woman's main roles should be maintaining a home and raising a family.

1964: The US Civil Rights Act of 1964 outlaws discrimination based on race, ethnicity, religion, sex, and national origin. The act also establishes the Equal Employment Opportunity Commission (EEOC) to enforce federal laws against discrimination in the workplace.

1968: Feminists stage a protest at the Miss America beauty pageant in Atlantic City, New Jersey, on the grounds that such pageants oppress women.

1970: Fifty thousand people march in the first Women's Strike for Equality in New York City.

1972: President Richard Nixon signs Title IX of the Education Amendments into law, outlawing gender discrimination in schools and educational programs that receive federal funding.

1975: President Gerald Ford signs a law requiring that women be admitted to the service academies of the US Army, Navy, Air Force, Merchant Marines, and Coast Guard.

1981: Sandra Day O'Connor becomes the first female justice on the US Supreme Court.

CHAPTER 6

LIFTOFF

AS SALLY RIDE AND HER CREWMATES MADE THEIR final preparations for the shuttle launch, more than 250,000 spectators jockeyed for spots along beaches, highways, and riverbanks near Cape Canaveral, Florida. Many wore T-shirts and buttons sporting the phrase RIDE, SALLY, RIDE, from the refrain of the 1966 Wilson Pickett hit "Mustang Sally." ("Ride Sally Ride" was also the title of a 1974 song by Lou Reed.) Meanwhile, some six hundred distinguished women from all walks of life gathered at a pre-liftoff reception sponsored by NASA. Gloria Steinem, cofounder of the groundbreaking feminist magazine *Ms.* was there. So were Liz Carpenter, a former aide to President Lyndon Johnson; Oscar-winning actress Jane Fonda; eight female members of Congress; and Jane Hart of the Mercury 13. "We understand that this is a milestone day in the space program," said

Brian Duff, director of public affairs for NASA. "We tried to invite a wide range of women who have made major contributions to the country."

Those who awakened early for the Saturday morning launch were treated to a warm, sunny day with all systems go for the mission. In fact, it would be one of the smoothest countdowns of the shuttle program, without a single delay. Once the crew arrived at the launch pad, they took an elevator ride up to the nose of the space shuttle *Challenger*, which was pointed skyward, 195 feet above the ground. From there they trod out onto a walkway similar to the Jetway people take from an airport terminal to board an airplane. Six technicians waited for the astronauts in the white room at the end of the walkway. The technicians helped the astronauts put on their launch helmets and climb through the hatch into the shuttle. Then they strapped the astronauts into their seats.

It was now 6:33 a.m. Over the next hour, the technicians went through one last checklist. They tested the radio system the astronauts would use to communicate with mission control. They made sure the paper, pencils, and manuals the crew would need during liftoff were nearby and anchored to something so they wouldn't float away.

They checked that oxygen was flowing into the astronauts' helmets. And they gave one final tug to be sure each crew member was strapped in tight. That was crucial because of the force of the launch they were about to experience. When everything passed muster, the technicians exited, shut the hatch, took the elevator down to the ground, and left the area. Soon afterward, the walkway and white room moved away from the shuttle, the astronauts closed the visors on their helmets, and the launch engines fired up. But not before mission control relayed a special message from Steve Hawley to his wife. "Sally, have a ball," he said over the radio. "See you Friday."

What happened next was something Sally would later describe in terms that many Americans could understand. "Have you ever been to Disneyland?" she asked CapCom Roy Bridges when he prodded her to give her impressions of the launch experience. Bridges said he had, and Sally proclaimed, "This is definitely an E ticket." At the time, Disneyland and Walt Disney World sold ticket books for their attractions. The tame, usually commercially sponsored rides were free. The next tier was A, followed by B, C, D, and finally E. E tickets were the most expensive and were assigned to the most elaborate, most thrilling attractions of all, such as, appropriately, Space Mountain.

Aboard the *Challenger*, the initial deafening, bone-shaking blast of the three launch engines quickly propelled the astronauts past the clouds and out of Earth's atmosphere. As the shuttle moved forward, the crew felt the power of its acceleration pushing them back against their seats. They were hit with a force of gravity ("g-force") three times as strong as that on Earth. "At first we don't mind it," Sally would later write. But, she added, "After a couple of minutes of 3 g's, we're uncomfortable, straining to hold our books on our laps and craning our necks against the force to read the instruments. I find myself wishing we'd hurry up and get into orbit."

Finally, eight and a half minutes after liftoff, the launch engines powered down and the crushing force was gone. Outside, the empty external fuel tank separated from the *Challenger*; it would soon burn up in the atmosphere. A few minutes later, the shuttle reached a distance of about fifty miles from Earth—about forty-three miles higher than commercial airplanes fly—and was officially in "space." But it needed a push from its internal engines to propel it to a comfortable orbit about two hundred miles above Earth. Once that was achieved, the shuttle maintained a speed of five miles per second—about three hundred times as fast as an automobile cruising down a highway. At that rate, the *Challenger* circled Earth once every ninety minutes, or sixteen times every day.

During liftoff, Sally served as flight engineer. She sat just behind the mission's commander, Bob Crippen, and the pilot, Rick Hauck, making sure they followed all the launch procedures and monitoring the shuttle's computers. When the *Challenger* settled into its orbit, Sally and the other astronauts removed their launch helmets and unbuckled the restraints that kept them in their seats. By that time, anything that wasn't battened down or otherwise secured was floating in the cabin, and the astronauts floated as well. It took them a while to get used to this new state of zero gravity, or weightlessness. The best way to move around was to push off the cabin's walls, but if they pushed too hard, they would slam into the opposite wall. "I soon learned to wind my way around with very gentle pushes," Sally would later write. She also figured out how to stop her body from drifting when she wanted to be still. "The only way to stop moving," she wrote, "is to take hold of something that's anchored in place."

While their bodies were getting used to zero gravity,

the *Challenger* crew started attending to the business at hand. In the cargo bay, the shuttle carried two communications satellites that would be deployed on behalf of other nations. The Anik C-2 would be launched to provide satellite television services in Canada, while the Palapa-B1 would improve telephone communications in Indonesia, the Philippines, Thailand, and other countries in Southeast Asia. Each satellite was less than ten feet long when stowed for launch, although it would telescope to about twenty-two feet once its antenna was raised and its solar panels moved into position. From the rear of the flight deck, Sally and John Fabian operated the controls that deployed the satellites, watching their progress on TV monitors and through windows that looked into the cargo bay. After launch, the satellites fired their solid rocket boosters to reach orbits about 22,300 miles from Earth.

Challenger also brought along two other major payloads. Sally's expertise with the Shuttle Remote Manipulator System (robot arm) would be important in deploying one of them, a West German satellite called SPAS-01 (for Shuttle Pallet Satellite). This satellite carried experiments designed to research the effects of microgravity (weak gravity) on the formation of different metal alloys (combinations of two or more metallic elements). Unlike the two communications satellites, the SPAS-01 would be released by the robot arm to fly alongside the *Challenger* for several hours. After that, the astronauts would use the robot arm to retrieve it so it could be brought back to Earth. Sally and John had spent a lot of time using the robot arm in simulations before the flight, so they were prepared. "The act of releasing a satellite and then backing the arm away felt very much like it did in the simulators," Sally would later say. "But the act of going up and capturing a satellite was a little more scary. I remember thinking, 'Oh, my gosh. This is real metal that will hit real metal if I miss. What if we don't capture the satellite?'" Fortunately, Sally's and John's disciplined training paid off. They had no problems reining in the SPAS-01.

NASA and the West German Ministry of Research and Technology worked together to develop the fourth payload. It was the first in a series planned for the shuttle program that would investigate how different materials were processed, or transformed, in space. Among the components on this mission was one that focused on how crystals grow in zero gravity.

These were just some of the onboard scientific studies

done during STS-7. Norm Thagard, who was a medical doctor, also conducted tests to explore the space motion sickness that some shuttle astronauts experienced while adapting to weightlessness. The crew spent a good deal of time observing and photographing Earth as well. Thanks to a camera on the SPAS-01, they were even able to take the first full image of the shuttle in space. "We spent a lot of time taking that picture," Sally would say. "We actually spent more time than we should have, much to mission control's surprise, putting the [robot] arm in the shape of a 7 before we took the picture so that everybody would know it was STS-7 that took it."

Between her other duties, Sally enjoyed looking out the window at planet Earth. "From space shuttle height, we can't see the entire globe at a glance, but we can look down the entire boot of Italy, or up the East Coast of the United States," she would later write. "The panoramic view inspires an appreciation for the scale of some of nature's phenomena." Shuttle astronauts were able to identify human-made features as well as natural ones, including cities, bridges, and airports. "A modern city like New York doesn't leap from the canvas of its surroundings," Sally would write, "but its straight piers and concrete runways

catch the eye—and around them, the city materializes."
She made a practice of "Earth-gazing" each day before she
went to sleep.

Over the course of their 147-hour mission, Sally and
the rest of the *Challenger* crew adapted to the joys and challenges of life in space. They ate three meals a day, combining
fresh food such as bread, apples, and cookies, with freeze-
dried and vacuum-packed casseroles and other entrées.
Astronauts took turns cooking, with one or two preparing
each meal for the whole crew. Cooking meant squirting
water into individual packages of food and placing them
in a convection oven, which used a fan to heat things faster
than a conventional oven. To serve the food, the astronaut
cook attached each person's meal tray to a wall with Velcro
and snugly fitted each item onto the tray. Crew members
carried their own utensils, which they wiped clean after
every meal and kept in their pockets. They used straws to
suck their drinks out of cartons because drinking glasses
did not work in space. The weightless liquid inside a glass
would stay put when the glass was tilted, or even turned
upside down.

There were no bathtubs or showers on the shuttle
because zero gravity would cause water droplets from the

faucets to float around the cabin. So to wash up, astronauts squirted water from a nozzle onto washcloths. The *Challenger*'s toilet, in a small closet on a wall of the cabin, looked a lot like an earthbound toilet, but it worked differently. On Earth, gravity pulls the urine and waste away from a person's body and down the toilet's bowl, where it rests until it is flushed into a drain pipe. Space toilets used air suction to pull the urine and waste into the bowl and down to a waste tank, where they were stored. The toilets also included leg restraints, to keep the astronaut from floating away before he or she was finished.

After a hard day's work, the shuttle astronauts had a variety of options on how—and where—to sleep. Some slept in sleeping bags with stiff pads that were attached to the cabin wall with Velcro. Others crawled into compartments that could be closed up like tiny bedrooms. Still others floated in the cabin, right side up, upside down, or sideways. Sally zipped herself up in a sleeping bag without the stiff pad and floated in a sitting position near one of the shuttle's windows. She didn't use a pillow because it would float away if it wasn't strapped to her head, and that was uncomfortable. No matter where and how they slept, though, all the astronauts wore black sleep masks. Every time the *Challenger* circled Earth, the astronauts witnessed one sunrise and one sunset. Since the shuttle circled Earth sixteen times a day, they had to contend with a sunrise every ninety minutes. Without a mask, the bright light could interfere with the soundest sleep.

STS-7 was scheduled to be the first shuttle mission to land at Kennedy Space Center in Florida, instead of Edwards Air Force Base in California. Landing in Florida would save NASA as much as $16 million, the cost of ferrying the ninety-five-ton shuttle across the country on top of a Boeing 747 jet. It also would allow a fast turnaround for the *Challenger*'s next mission, which was scheduled for August 16, just two months away. On Friday morning, June 24, NASA was ready to roll out the red carpet in Florida to welcome the astronauts home. Sally's parents had flown in from California for the event, and the families of Bob Crippen, Rick Hauck, John Fabian, and Norm Thagard were there as well. President Ronald Reagan was set to fly in to greet the astronauts too. But the weather did not cooperate. It was raining in Florida, and the Kennedy Space Center was socked in by fog, so the *Challenger* headed to California. Instead of arriving to great fanfare and crowds of supporters, the astronauts were met by a handful of excited well-wishers and several hundred Edwards Air Force Base employees.

President Reagan did telephone the crew about three hours after they landed. He declared that their mission was "just a most thrilling thing, and I can't tell you how much we are proud of you." Then he spoke directly to Sally. "Your handling of that long arm and that retrieval and all," he said, "did indicate that you were there for one reason: because you were the best person for the job." While Sally graciously accepted the president's compliments, she did not accept a large bouquet of white carnations and roses offered to her at a ceremony when the crew returned to Houston. "She had said before the six-day mission that she wanted to be treated no differently than her four crewmates," reported the *Washington Post*. So she shook her head when a NASA official offered her the flowers. The *Post* also noted that while the wives of the four male astronauts each received a single red rose at the ceremony, Sally's husband, Steve, did not.

Despite her best intentions, Sally was treated differently from her crewmates. The end of the STS-7 mission brought a flurry of requests for interviews and public appearances her way. "While I was training, I had been protected from it all," Sally would later say. "But the moment we landed, that protective shield was gone. . . . Everybody wanted a piece of me after the flight." In the months that followed, Sally's life was a whirlwind of speeches, news conferences, rallies, and luncheons. But on November 17, 1983, she got the excuse she needed to curtail her public appearances. That day, NASA released the list of crew members for eleven upcoming shuttle missions, and her name was on it. "Thank goodness," Sally would later say. "Back into training, safe again."

CHAPTER 7

RETURN TRIP

WHEN SALLY RIDE GOT THE NEWS THAT SHE WOULD be returning to space, there was little of the fanfare that had accompanied the announcement of her first mission. "I actually don't remember the details of how I found out about this second flight assignment," Sally would later say. "It was George Abbey, again, who told us, but I really don't remember the details." In fact, unlike her first flight, Sally was not singled out and told about the mission before her crewmates; all of them learned about it at the same time.

Sally's second mission had a crew of seven people—the largest team to date for a shuttle flight. Bob Crippen was again named commander, but this time his pilot was Jon McBride, a decorated navy veteran. Besides Sally, there were two other mission specialists, including one of the other women from her astronaut class, geologist Kathryn Sullivan.

The third mission specialist was David Leestma, an aeronautical engineer and a commander in the navy. They would be accompanied by two payload specialists, people chosen and trained by research companies or other nations to supervise the work with specific payloads. In that role, Marc Garneau, a naval commander and an electrical engineer, would be the first Canadian to venture into space. Oceanographer Paul Scully-Power, who worked with the Royal Australian and US navies, would be the first Australian.

Newspaper reports pointed out that this was the first shuttle crew to include two female astronauts, but the spotlight continued to shine on NASA's First Woman. "Sally was still right in the bull's-eye of all the media interest," Kathryn Sullivan would remember. "The flight was announced all of about five or six months after her first landing, so there's still a flood of interest surrounding her." Some members of the media were so single-minded that they behaved rather badly. During publicity events, Kathryn said, "people would come at me, and they didn't actually really want to talk to me. They wanted to know where Sally was." The experience helped stoke a friendly rivalry between the two astronauts. Kathryn gave Sally a certain amount of ribbing about being the media's darling and finally started wearing a name tag at work that said EVIDENTLY WHAT I AM IS "NOT SALLY."

Although this would be the thirteenth shuttle mission, NASA was reluctant to label a flight with the number thirteen. Superstitious fears that the number brought bad luck seemed to have been borne out by the disastrous problems that befell NASA's Apollo 13 flight in 1970. About fifty-six hours after that moon mission was launched, an oxygen tank onboard exploded, causing a fire. The fire crippled the ship's service module, and that severely limited power in the command module, which housed the three-man crew. The men were forced to abort their planned moon landing and live in the ship's lunar module until they were close enough to reenter Earth's orbit. (The lunar module was the small vehicle meant to ferry two Apollo astronauts to the moon's surface and back.) The crew returned safely, but NASA didn't want to tempt fate.

Starting in 1984, NASA instituted a new numbering system that designated Sally's second flight STS-41G. As before, the STS stood for Space Transportation System. The "4" indicated the year of the mission, 1984. The "1" meant the flight would be launched from the number one launch site, the Kennedy Space Center (as opposed to

Vandenberg Air Force Base in California, site 2). And the G indicated the flight's order on the schedule for that year. (The first flight of the year was labeled *A*.) To make the system even more confusing, missions that were delayed or canceled kept the numbers they were originally assigned.

Bob Crippen was scheduled to command STS-41C before he could start training for 41G. Since Sally was the only other member of the 41G crew who had previously flown a shuttle mission, and since she had already worked with Crip, she played the unofficial role of second in command. "Part of my job was to say, 'This is the way Crip likes to handle this situation or this sort of problem,'" Sally later remembered. "I tried to give the rest of the crew some indication of the way that Crip likes to run a flight and run a crew." During launch and reentry simulations, Kathryn or David Leestma filled in as commander, while Sally and Jon McBride went over their duties as flight engineer and pilot, respectively. Crip joined them after 41C completed its mission in April 1984, giving him close to six months to train for the October 5 launch of 41G.

Once again, Sally's voyage in space would be aboard the *Challenger*, which was embarking on its sixth mission in two years. NASA's directors had ambitious plans for the shuttle program, aiming to launch one flight per month through 1985, and then sixteen flights in 1986. So far they were on track. The space shuttle *Discovery* began its maiden voyage on August 30, giving NASA a fleet of three working space vehicles, including *Columbia*. Now, exactly one month after *Discovery*'s return, the 41G crew was strapped into their seats on *Challenger*, ready for their predawn liftoff.

The Shuttle Fleet

Over the course of its thirty-year history, the shuttle program used five different orbiter vehicles (OVs). Missions never overlapped; one was finished before the next one began. But the presence of numerous orbiters allowed for a more compact schedule of launches. Despite NASA's goal of monthly launches, though, there would never be more than nine shuttle launches in a calendar year.

Columbia

- **NAMED FOR:** Privately owned American fur-trading ship *Columbia* of the late eighteenth century, as well as the term historically used for the United States of America

- **FIRST MISSION:** STS-1, April 1981

- **LAST MISSION:** STS-107, January 2003 (disintegrated during reentry)

- **TOTAL MISSIONS:** 28

Challenger

- **NAMED FOR:** HMS *Challenger*, the British command ship on a nineteenth-century marine research expedition

- **FIRST MISSION:** STS-6, April 1983

- **LAST MISSION:** STS-51L, January 1986 (disintegrated after launch)

- **TOTAL MISSIONS:** 10

Discovery

- **NAMED FOR:** Four British exploring ships named HMS *Discovery*, especially one commanded by Captain James Cook from 1776 to 1779

- **FIRST MISSION:** STS-41D, August 1984

- **LAST MISSION:** STS-133, February 2011

- **TOTAL MISSIONS:** 39

Atlantis

- **NAMED FOR:** R/V *Atlantis*, a two-masted, twentieth-century sailing ship that was a research vessel for the Woods Hole Oceanographic Institution in Massachusetts

- **FIRST MISSION:** STS-51J, October 1985

- **LAST MISSION:** STS-135, July 2011 (last shuttle mission ever)

- **TOTAL MISSIONS:** 33

Endeavour

- **NAMED FOR:** British Captain James Cook's ship HMS *Endeavour*

- **FIRST MISSION:** STS-49, May 1992
- **LAST MISSION:** STS-134, May 2011
- **TOTAL MISSIONS:** 25

Looking back at the launch of this eight-day mission, Sally would say she "had very much the same experience the second time as the first." No doubt Commander Crippen's track record had something to do with that. This was his fourth shuttle mission, making him the most experienced shuttle astronaut at NASA. Although Crip had wondered if packing seven people into the shuttle's cabin constituted overcrowding, he was quick to change his mind. After the *Challenger* had entered an orbit 218 miles from Earth, the crew pushed themselves out of their seats and floated in front of the TV cameras that were sending images back home. "You really can get seven in here," he said. "Everybody is having fun."

Before long, the astronauts stopped horsing around and got to work. On day one, Sally used the shuttle's robot arm to deploy the Earth Radiation Budget Satellite (ERBS). This 5,087-pound spacecraft contained instruments that would provide scientific data about the chemical makeup of the ozone layer and other parts of Earth's atmosphere.

(The ozone layer is the part of the atmosphere that stops dangerous radiation from the sun from reaching Earth's surface.) As it turned out, launching the satellite required more finesse than Sally expected. Metal hinges on the solar panels had become stuck in the cold environment of space, so Sally used the robot arm to shake the ERBS until the panels moved into place. After that was done, the satellite's thrusters propelled it to an orbit three hundred fifty miles above Earth. Scientists hoped they would be able to collect data from the ERBS for two years. In the end, it would provide valuable information for more than two decades.

Among its other payloads, *Challenger* carried a Shuttle Imaging Radar-B (SIR-B) system, which would be the centerpiece of forty-four different investigations touching on archeology, geology, cartography, oceanography, and botany. At the heart of SIR-B was an eight-panel antenna that would be stowed in the payload bay during launch and landing. The antenna opened up to a span measuring thirty-five feet by seven feet. When it was pointed at Earth, it would transmit millions of radar pulses that would record detailed images of terrain on the planet. Using this technology, scientists hoped to search for evidence of early human life in the deserts of Egypt and the Sudan, find

Nordic ruins on the Swedish island of Öland, and much more. But the antenna would have to be folded up temporarily during the flight. Otherwise, it would interfere with another highlight of the 41G mission, an extravehicular activity (EVA), or space walk, by Kathryn Sullivan and David Leestma.

Folding up the antenna turned out to be a problem that Sally and the robot arm were called upon to solve. "Under normal circumstances, the Imaging Radar would have had nothing to do with the arm at all," Sally would say. "But we had trouble folding it—we couldn't get it to come down all the way to the latch." So they improvised. "We set the [robot] arm down on top of one of the leaves of the antenna and pushed down on it," Sally said. Finally the latch snapped shut. "If we hadn't been able to do that, the space walk might have been canceled. But it worked quite well."

Thanks to this maneuver, on the fifth day of the mission, Kathryn and David left the shuttle for three hours to test the Orbital Refueling System (ORS). The ORS would allow astronauts to transfer additional fuel to working satellites that were running low, like filling up the gas tank of a car.* If successful, the refueling effort would extend the lives of satellites that would otherwise be abandoned in space. For this trial run, Kathryn and David worked on a simulated satellite fuel tank. They used special tools to attach a one-way valve to the tank and then strung a hose from the *Challenger* to the valve. The following day, when the astronauts were safe inside the shuttle, an actual transfer of the toxic hydrazine would take place.

Prior to ending their space walk, Kathryn and David also did some repair work on the *Challenger*. They secured the vehicle's communications antenna, which had been wobbling loosely. And Kathryn checked out the problematic SIR-B antenna. Her observations convinced mission control that if the antenna was opened up again, the astronauts would be able to snap it closed. "Before long we're back in, popping out of the suits, and everyone's happy," Kathryn remembered in 2008. "It's amazing. It is just a really fabulously cool experience. . . . Only a small number of folks ever get to fly in space in the era of history that we've come along in, and only about a quarter or so of those ever get to sneak outside."

---

* While most satellites use solar energy to run their electronics and communications systems, they use a liquid fuel called hydrazine to power the engines that keep them in the right orbit.

While the technical glitches on 41G were annoying, the crew accomplished much of what they set out to do. The transfer of fuel to the simulated satellite worked. A special Large Format Camera (LFC) sent back 2,300 detailed photographs that monitored and mapped the Earth's surface. The success of the Shuttle Imaging Radar convinced NASA to go ahead with plans to launch a radar probe to map the planet Venus before the end of the decade. And during the mission, the astronauts had shot footage with an IMAX camera that would be part of a film about the space shuttle program called *The Dream Is Alive.*

As 41G headed home, however, there was one more goal to achieve. Like STS-7, this mission was set to land at the Kennedy Space Center in Florida. Commander Crippen had been forced to divert to Edwards Air Force Base in California on both STS-7 and his most recent flight, STS-41C. But finally conditions were right for a Florida landing. "The third time is the charm," Crip told mission control when he heard the news. After flying 13.5 million miles, the commander charted the *Challenger's* course for Runway 33, a three-mile-long concrete airstrip at the Shuttle Landing Facility in Brevard County, Florida. The shuttle fired its thrusters over Australia, headed toward

Alaska and Canada, then flew over the Midwest with Florida in its sights. It landed at 12:26 p.m. Eastern Daylight Time on October 13, only three miles from where it had taken off eight days before.

On STS-41G, Sally became the first American woman to travel to space twice. And Kathryn Sullivan became the first American woman to take a space walk. After the mission, the media were anxious to speak to *both* of these pioneering women. "There was a fair amount of attention," Sally would remember. "But it was manageable. It really wasn't nearly as intense as it was after STS-7." Once again, though, Sally's public obligations were curtailed when she received another space shuttle assignment. NASA was approaching its ambitious goal of sending one shuttle up each month, and the agency needed its iconic astronaut back in space. Sally would be one of five crew members— and the only woman—on STS-61I, set to launch as early as July 15, 1986.

Sally's newest mission would be her third trip on the *Challenger*. Before that, though, the orbiter would undertake another high-profile journey that had captured the public's attention. Christa McAuliffe, a high school social studies teacher from New Hampshire, was selected from more than eleven thousand applicants to be America's first "teacher in space." As the first ordinary citizen to travel aboard the shuttle, Christa would symbolize how accessible space travel had become. In late January and early February 1986, she was scheduled to teach lessons that would be broadcast into American classrooms from the *Challenger* during mission STS-51L. But then the unthinkable happened. Seventy-three seconds after takeoff on January 28, 1986, the *Challenger* exploded, killing all seven men and women onboard.

CHAPTER 8

DISASTER

IT WAS LATE MORNING ON TUESDAY, JANUARY 28, 1986, and Sally Ride was on a commercial airplane flying to Houston, Texas. At the Kennedy Space Center in Florida, seven astronauts were strapped into their seats aboard the *Challenger*, ready to lift off for NASA's twenty-fifth space shuttle mission, STS-51L. Four of the crew were members of Sally's 1978 astronaut class: Judith Resnik, Ronald McNair, Ellison Onizuka, and commander Francis "Dick" Scobee. The pilot, Michael Smith, joined the astronaut corps in 1980. Gregory Jarvis, an engineer with Hughes Aircraft, was a payload specialist on the mission. So was Christa McAuliffe, the high school teacher who had trained with the crew for close to six months.

Before this, Sally had watched every shuttle launch since the first one in 1981 as it happened, either in person or on TV. But this mission had been rescheduled or scrubbed five times, first because of the delayed takeoff of the previous shuttle flight and then because of bad weather. Now, as Sally sat on the airplane, the pilot's voice came over the intercom with a startling announcement. There had been an accident on the *Challenger*, he said. No one was certain of the details or whether the crew had been hurt. Sally was out of her seat in an instant. "I pulled out my NASA badge and went up to the cockpit," she would remember. "They let me put on an extra pair of headsets to monitor the radio traffic to find out what had happened. We were only about half an hour outside of Houston. When we landed, I headed straight back to the Astronaut Office at JSC [Johnson Space Center]."

Sally quickly learned that the accident had been cata-strophic and none of the crew had survived. The *Challenger* was only about ten miles from Earth when Commander Dick Scobee heeded mission control's direction to open up the shuttle's throttle, sending fuel to its engines. "Roger, go with throttle up," confirmed the commander. Then Americans, including thousands of schoolchildren who had tuned in to watch a teacher journey to space, saw the worst kind of history play out on their TVs. Soaring against a clear blue sky, the shuttle suddenly exploded into a burst of flames, followed by two divergent trails of smoke. NASA's public affairs officer, Steve Nesbitt, who had been narrating the launch from mission control in Houston, paused a moment before declaring, "Flight controllers here looking very carefully at the situation. Obviously a major malfunction."

It fell to President Ronald Reagan to try and comfort the stunned nation. In doing so, he directly addressed the children who had witnessed the tragedy. "I know it's hard to understand that sometimes painful things like this happen," he said. "It's all part of the process of exploration and discovery. It's all part of taking a chance and expanding man's horizons. The future doesn't belong to the faint-hearted, it belongs to the brave. The *Challenger* crew was pulling us into the future and we'll continue to follow them." The president was scheduled to deliver his annual State of the Union address that evening, but he postponed it a week. In all of the nation's history, the State of the Union had never been delayed before.

NASA suspended all future shuttle flights indefinitely while the accident was thoroughly investigated. That investigation was conducted by a group appointed by President Reagan. The Presidential Commission on the Space Shuttle Challenger Accident was chaired by William P. Rogers, who had served as secretary of state under President Richard Nixon and as attorney general under President Dwight D. Eisenhower. The vice chair was Neil Armstrong, the retired astronaut who had become the first man to walk on the moon during the Apollo 11 mission in 1969. The thirteen-member group, which came to be known as the Rogers Commission, included physicists, engineers, attorneys, and military aviators. The only active astronaut on the commission, and the only woman, was Sally Ride.

President Reagan gave the commission 120 days to conduct its investigation and share its findings. Sally went to Washington DC for the group's first meeting and stayed until their final report was completed in early June. The commission called witnesses to testify before them in Washington. They also traveled around the country to interview officials at NASA offices and the headquarters of contractors that had helped build the shuttle. In all, they conducted more than thirty-five formal hearings and interviewed more than 160 individuals. The transcripts from those hearings and interviews totaled almost twelve thousand pages and covered everything from NASA's management structure to the specifics of the *Challenger*'s design. The commissioners also examined hundreds of photographs and gathered 6,300 additional documents totaling more than 122,000 pages.

Throughout this time, Sally used the importance of her work on the commission to move forward from the devastating experience of losing her friends and fellow astronauts. "I was just going from day to day and just grinding through all the data that we had to grind through," she remembered in 2002. "But it was a very, very difficult time. It was a difficult time for me and a difficult time for all the other astronauts, for all the reasons that you might expect. It was very, very hard on all of us. You could see it in our faces in the months that followed the accident."

As the only active astronaut on the Rogers Commission, Sally provided firsthand information on NASA's procedures for shuttle launches. She also chaired a subcommittee that looked into other aspects of shuttle flights, such as the training that astronauts received. But she spent most of her time as part of the larger panel, looking for the technical cause of the accident and determining how that flaw went unnoticed by NASA officials. "The panel, by and large, functioned as a unit," she said. "We held hearings; we jointly decided what we should look into, what witnesses should be called before the panel, and where the hearings should be held."

Ultimately, the commission's 256-page report found that the explosion of the *Challenger* centered on one of the shuttle's two solid rocket boosters. These reusable rockets provided most of the power during the first two minutes of the shuttle's launch. Then they detached and fell into the ocean, where they were recovered. On STS-51L, a rubbery joint—called an O-ring—between the two lower segments of the shuttle's right solid rocket booster failed. "The specific failure was the destruction of the seals that are intended to prevent hot gases from leaking through the joint during the propellant burn of the rocket motor," stated the report. "The evidence assembled by the Commission indicates that no other element of the Space Shuttle system contributed to this failure."

While the O-ring was the physical cause, however, the report went on to identify management issues at NASA and one of its contractors that eventually led to the *Challenger* tragedy. "The Space Shuttle's Solid Rocket Booster problem began with the faulty design of its joint," read the commission's report, "and increased as both NASA and contractor management first failed to recognize it as a problem, then failed to fix it and finally treated it as an acceptable flight risk." In fact, engineers at NASA had identified possible problems with the O-rings as early as 1977, when the space shuttle was being designed. But Morton Thiokol, the company that made the solid rocket boosters, did not feel there was a significant flaw. And managers at the NASA facility in Huntsville, Alabama, which oversaw the building of the shuttle, downplayed the concerns of their own engineers about these seals. They did not even share those concerns with NASA head-quarters in Washington DC.

Once space shuttle missions began, engineers at NASA found varying degrees of damage to the O-rings of used solid rocket boosters. They determined that there was more damage in colder weather because the rubber in the O-rings got stiff in the cold and could not function prop-erly. On January 28, 1986, the temperature at the shuttle launch site was at least fifteen degrees colder than the temperature at any previous launch. In other words, the conditions were ripe for catastrophe.

In light of their findings, the Rogers Commission issued a list of recommendations to ensure that another shuttle tragedy would never occur. They started with the redesign and careful testing of all solid rocket booster joints and seals. They also called for a review of the way the shuttle program was managed, suggesting that former astronauts be moved into management positions at NASA so they could share their expertise. And they called for better communications throughout NASA.

When the grueling work on the Rogers Commission was done, Sally had a decision to make. She had been planning to leave NASA after her third mission, to go back to doing physics research at a university. But all shuttle flights still were grounded, and the future of the program seemed unclear. In the summer of 1986, Sally accepted that she would not travel to space a third time. However, she didn't feel right about leaving the agency in the aftermath of the *Challenger* tragedy. "I decided to stay at NASA for an extra year," she said. "I wanted to stay a while to help the recovery process." (Ultimately, NASA would resume its shuttle missions in September 1988.)

Sally accepted a new assignment at NASA headquarters in Washington as assistant administrator for long-range and strategic planning. In that position, she conducted research throughout NASA to develop a plan for the organization's future. In August 1987 she issued a sixty-three-page report titled *Leadership and America's Future in Space*, which came to be called the Ride Report. It identified four major projects for the space agency. They were the study of Earth's atmosphere and environment using satellites; unmanned scientific missions to study the comets, asteroids, and planets in our outer solar system; building a permanent outpost on the moon; and human spaceflights to Mars, with an eventual permanent base there as well.

While working on the Ride Report, Sally became the director of a new department at NASA, the Office of Exploration. This office was tasked with producing studies and plans focused on human exploration of the moon and Mars. Sally worked to set up the department, but then she announced that she was moving on. She had been offered a position as a science fellow at Stanford University's Center for International Security and Arms Control. This center, founded in 1983, focused on security problems between nations. Through education and research, the center aimed to influence the officials who created policies on topics such as arms control and international cooperation.

Following in Sally's Footsteps

Although Sally and the five other women in the class of 1978 were America's first female astronauts, they were hardly the last. Between 1983 and 2013, forty-four American women flew in space. Among the others were:

- **MAE JEMISON**, the first African-American woman in space, STS-47, September 1992

- **ELLEN OCHOA**, the first Hispanic woman in space, STS-56, April 1993

- **EILEEN COLLINS**, the first female shuttle pilot, STS-63, February 1995, and the first female shuttle commander, STS-93, July 1999

- **PAMELA MELROY**, the second female shuttle commander, STS-120, October 2007

- **BARBARA MORGAN**, the first educator astronaut, STS-118, August 2007. (She had been Christa McAuliffe's backup in the Teacher in Space program, but ultimately trained as a full-fledged astronaut.)

- **PEGGY WHITSON**, the first female commander of the International Space Station, October 2007; the most experienced female astronaut with just over 376 days in space

As Sally's professional life changed, so did her personal life. She and Steve Hawley divorced in 1987 as she grew closer to Tam O'Shaughnessy, a woman she'd known since they were both twelve years old. Like Sally, Tam had been a tennis player. She'd even gone on to become a pro, playing on the women's tennis circuit for several years. She had some success, winning a national women's doubles title (with partner Pam Austin) in 1969, but then she left the circuit to continue her education. Tam earned bachelor's and master's degrees in biology from Georgia State University and a PhD in school psychology from the University of California, Riverside. Her research centered on helping kids who had reading problems.

As always, Sally kept her personal life private. But she shared Tam's interest in educating young people and was especially eager to influence kids to pursue careers in science, technology, engineering, and math (collectively known as STEM). In 1986 she had partnered with reporter Susan Okie to write *To Space & Back*, a book for kids ages ten and up. It offered a behind-the-scenes look at a space shuttle flight and was packed with the vivid details only a shuttle veteran could offer. "I'd been doing a lot of speaking, and it was really obvious that kids are fascinated by the space program," she said. "The book is a good way to encourage their interest in science and teach them a little bit while they're not looking."

It turned out that Sally had stumbled onto a new career path while *she* wasn't looking. She began to think about the teachers who had fostered her love of math and science, such as Elizabeth Mommaerts. Sally wanted to make sure all kids—and especially all girls—had the chance to engage in science careers if they wanted to. She realized that her position as the first American woman in space made her the perfect person to reach out to girls and show them how exciting and challenging science could be. Guiding future generations of scientists and engineers might not be as physically challenging as surviving 3 g's or as thrilling as witnessing a sunrise every ninety minutes, but it was a meaningful goal for Sally. "A lot of girls start to lose that self-esteem, lose that self-confidence in middle school," she said. "For me, it was later and I was . . . very fortunate that I had some influential teachers to help me through that." As the end of the twentieth century approached, Sally got ready to pay it forward.

CHAPTER 9

IMAGINARY LINES

IN THE EARLY 1980S, WOMEN AND MINORITIES started using a new term to describe a barrier that seemed to be stopping them from rising to the top jobs in corporate America. The term was the "glass ceiling." They could see those high-paying, high-profile jobs. But there seemed to be an invisible barrier making them impossible to attain.

As Sally Ride settled into life after NASA, she gave a lot of thought to glass ceilings and what was keeping women out of science and engineering careers. She decided the problem began with the messages girls who loved science and math got when they were in school. "If a girl who's twelve says she wants to be an electrical engineer, she gets a slightly different reaction . . . than a twelve-year-old boy who says that he wants to be an electrical engineer," she said. "Sometimes these signals are very subtle, but kids are pretty smart and they start to pick up on them. And the result is that starting in about middle school . . . more girls than boys start to drift away from math and science."

After she left NASA, Sally shared her enthusiasm about science on two fronts. First, she continued to teach college students. In 1989 Sally left Stanford University to fill two positions at the University of California, San Diego (UCSD). She became a professor of physics as well as the director of the university's California Space Institute, nicknamed CalSpace. Besides teaching, she conducted research and wrote scholarly papers related to the free electron lasers she had studied in graduate school. At CalSpace, she directed research centered on the ways space technology could be used to study global climate change.

While she was doing cutting-edge physics, Sally also was writing books on science topics for kids. For these books, her coauthor was Tam O'Shaughnessy. After the success of *To Space & Back*, Sally said, a publisher "called me out of the blue and asked me to do another book for kids—this one on the Voyager spacecraft." In 1977, NASA had launched two unmanned Voyager space probes meant to provide images and information about the planets Jupiter and Saturn. They completed their original missions in 1989, then continued to transmit information as they neared Uranus and Neptune. Sally and Tam wrote *Voyager: An Adventure to the Edge of the Solar System* in 1992, but the probes were still sending back information as late as 2013. In September of that year, scientists declared *Voyager I* to be the farthest human-made object ever sent from Earth, having traveled some 11.7 billion miles. They also confirmed it to be the first human-made object to leave our solar system and enter interstellar space.*

Sally and Tam wrote two other books in the 1990s. In 1994, they collaborated on *The Third Planet: Exploring Earth from Space*. In 1999 they wrote *The Mystery of Mars*. Meanwhile, Sally created an innovative program at CalSpace that gave middle school students the chance to take part in shuttle missions—while still having their feet planted firmly on the ground. KidSat was first tested in 1996 aboard STS-76. (Shuttle missions went back to their original numbering system after the *Challenger* explosion.) The program allowed middle school students to direct a camera to take photographs from space of specific locations on Earth. "We fly a digital camera in the crew cabin

---

* Interstellar space is the previously unexplored dark region beyond the charged particles surrounding our solar system.

of the shuttle," Sally explained. "The astronauts mount that camera so that it points to the Earth, and then we control the camera from the ground. The camera is actually controlled by middle school students from their classrooms via the World Wide Web through a control center at UCSD." KidSat flew on six shuttle missions and then became a permanent payload on the International Space Station (ISS).* In 1998 KidSat was renamed EarthKAM (for Earth Knowledge Acquired by Middle school students). In 2013 NASA renamed the program Sally Ride EarthKAM.

Not long after she launched KidSat, Sally stepped down from her position as director of CalSpace. She planned to concentrate on teaching and research, but her interest in educating the public—especially kids—about space and the environment led her down a different path. In the spring of 1999, Sally heard that former CNN television anchor Lou Dobbs was planning to start an Internet business called Space.com. "The vision at the time was to create a website that catered to everyone who had an interest in space—for whatever reason," she said. "It would be for kids interested in the space program, people who loved

---

* The ISS is a large spacecraft orbiting about 220 miles above Earth. It has been used cooperatively by fifteen nations since 2000 for research and exploration.

science fiction, the commercial aerospace community—everyone." Sally loved the idea of a reliable, easy-to-access source of news and information about the space program and contacted Dobbs to tell him so. He ended up convincing her to take a leave of absence from her teaching position at UCSD to work for the website. She joined the board of directors and soon became president of the company.

Space.com's headquarters were in New York City, so Sally flew from San Diego at the beginning of each week and returned home on weekends. While she was in New York, she stayed in a hotel. It was a grueling commute and after about a year and a half, Sally decided to resign. She considered going back to teaching, but her experiences at this start-up venture had inspired another idea. "I started thinking more and more about doing something that was focused more on girls and education than Space.com," she said. "I started talking with my friends and several of us decided to form Imaginary Lines."

Imaginary Lines, Inc., aimed to capture the enthusiasm that middle school girls had for science and math before they were discouraged from pursuing scientific careers. "What drove me to start the company," Sally told the

New York Times, "was the sense that a lot of the stereo-types about girls and science and math that we all assumed would be gone by now, have not gone away." The name of the company, which she founded with Tam and others in 2001, was partly a nod to the barriers women faced in their professional lives. "We wanted a name that had some allusion to science but that also had an allusion to glass ceilings and to the imaginary lines that can connect girls to each other and to women," said Sally.

Since her history-making journey into space years earlier, Sally had been determined not to exploit her achievements for financial gain. As a NASA employee, she was prohibited from making any money beyond her salary, which was $42,653 in 1983. But after she retired from the space program in 1987, she was free to pursue any endorsements that came her way. And agents were anxious to work with her. "Her exploits as the first US female astronaut in space can earn her a great deal of money," said Kent Stanner of the International Management Group, a company that managed the careers of top athletes. "She's a natural for endorsing health foods, women's athletic clothes, jogging shoes, helmets, airlines, the whole works." Another agent, Norman Brokaw of the William Morris Agency, predicted that Sally could make a million dollars her first year out of NASA. Yet she rejected almost all endorsement offers. She also turned down requests to write a memoir or to have her life portrayed in a motion picture, though Jane Fonda was interested in playing her.

When it came to Imaginary Lines, however, Sally was willing to use her fame. "I felt that this was something that was really worth using my name and using the visibility that I could bring to it," she said in 2002. "It felt worthwhile." The business focused on creating science-related events, programs, and activities that appealed to girls. "We're doing summer science camps for girls," said Sally. "We're doing one-day festivals—science festivals for middle school girls at college campuses around the country." Girls who attended the camps and festivals worked on exciting science projects at workshops with titles such as Bat Mania, Bottle Rocket Madness, and Enzyme Magic. They also met female scientists and engineers including ocean explorer Dr. Sylvia Earle and astronaut Ellen Ochoa, who could inspire them to follow in their footsteps. And they met other girls who thought science was cool. "We're getting a great reaction to our events and activities, both from the girls and from their parents,"

Sally said. "We think that the time is right for this."

In 2002 the company announced its first TOYchallenge, a toy and game design competition for students in grades five through eight. This national competition tasked teams of students, with an adult coach, to invent toys or games. The TOYchallenge was open to both boys and girls, but at least half the members of each team had to be girls. The contest attracted 243 teams in its initial season.

For the regional level of the TOYchallenge, teams had to choose a theme from one of several toy categories (such as "Games for the Family" and "Remarkable Robots") and brainstorm ideas. Then they had to develop a written description, a visual presentation, and an early model of their toy or game. Those moving on to the national level had to build a prototype, or working model, of their design. Entries were judged on originality, feasibility, the description of the design process, and team participation, among other criteria. Winners got prizes such as trips to Space Camp or action figures designed in their likeness by Hasbro, a contest sponsor. "Our TOYchallenge contest encapsulates our philosophy that science is fun," said Sally in 2007. "Whether you're building a toy or a bridge, you employ the same principles. The TOY challenge is engineering in disguise."

With its camps, festivals, and TOY challenges, Imaginary Lines quickly laid the groundwork for successful programs that would, as Sally said, "put a female face on math and science." At the same time, she and Tam continued to write books together. Their next volume, *Exploring Our Solar System*, was scheduled to be published in the fall of 2003. But before then, Sally was pulled away from the business of making science fun to answer a more somber call. On February 1, 2003, tragedy once again struck the space shuttle program, and NASA needed Sally to help them figure out why.

CHAPTER 10

LEADING THE WAY

COMMANDER RICK HUSBAND AND THE CREW OF STS-107 had been conducting scientific studies around the clock for more than fifteen days aboard the space shuttle *Columbia*. On Saturday morning, February 1, 2003, almost twenty years since Sally's first flight, the shuttle was heading for a landing at the Kennedy Space Center. The weather was beautiful in Florida, but the waiting crowds never got to welcome the astronauts home.

At nine a.m., about sixteen minutes before the shuttle's scheduled landing time, the vehicle disintegrated some thirty-nine miles above Earth. The crew perished as fiery debris rained down on East Texas, western Louisiana, and southwestern Arkansas. The wreckage tore holes in rooftops and scarred lawns and parking lots, but miraculously, no one on the ground was injured or killed. (However, two men would be killed and three would be injured in a helicopter crash during the subsequent search for debris.)

Columbia, the oldest space shuttle, was on its twenty-eighth mission. The crew consisted of five men and two women, the same configuration that was onboard the *Challenger* when it exploded in 1986. Commander Husband, an air force colonel, was on his second shuttle mission, having served as the pilot on STS-96 four years before. The pilot on this flight was William C. McCool, a commander in the US Navy. There were three mission specialists: David M. Brown and Laurel B. Clark, who were both flight surgeons and captains in the navy, and Kalpana Chawla, an engineer born in India who was on her second mission. Michael P. Anderson, a physicist and a lieutenant colonel in the air force, also was on his second shuttle mission and served as payload commander. And Ilan Ramon, a colonel in the Israeli Air Force, was a payload specialist and the first Israeli to travel in space.

Following the *Challenger* disaster in 1986, NASA had adopted procedures to form an independent panel to investigate any space-related accident that occurred. Less than two hours after the loss of *Columbia*, NASA's administrator, Sean O'Keefe, announced a Columbia Accident

Investigation Board (CAIB). The board would be headed by retired admiral Harold W. Gehman Jr., of the US Navy. Among the first things the admiral did was to work with O'Keefe to guarantee that the nine-member board truly was independent of NASA's influence and would give an honest, unbiased assessment. He also addressed the concerns of critics who noted that the board members were mainly from NASA, the military, and the US Department of Transportation. Over the next several weeks, Admiral Gehman added four more committee members who were scientists and professors. Among them was Sally Ride.

Sally was the only person to serve on both the Presidential Commission on the Space Shuttle Challenger Accident and the Columbia Accident Investigation Board. Her singular experience made her a valuable member of the *Columbia* group. During her six months on the CAIB, at hearings held in Texas, Florida, and Washington DC, she was quick to observe troubling similarities between the two shuttle tragedies. "There are many parallels," she told the *New York Times* that August. "Not so much between the accidents themselves, but between some of the organizational contributing causes to the accidents. One parallel is that before the *Challenger* accident there were several shuttle flights where the first stages of the problem were seen."

In the case of the *Columbia*, the problem was that a chunk of foam insulation about the size of a brief-case broke off the shuttle's external fuel tank during its launch on January 16. The chunk then hit the leading edge of the shuttle's left wing, causing a breach (break) in *Columbia*'s thermal protection system. That system was meant to protect the shuttle from the extreme temperatures it would encounter upon reentering Earth's atmosphere. Because of the breach, the superheated air broke through the protection system during reentry and melted the aluminum in the left wing. Without the wing, the vehicle was weakened and the crew lost control as it flew through the air at 12,500 miles per hour. Finally the shuttle broke apart.

Just as *Challenger* had experienced O-ring problems before 1986, foam problems were nothing new to *Columbia*. The CAIB's final report listed thirteen instances of "significant Thermal Protection System damage or major foam loss" for space shuttle vehicles before 2003, including seven for *Columbia*. Yet NASA did not treat the foam issue with urgency. "There was never a real significant engineering effort to understand why this was happening," said Sally. "There was no catastrophic damage the first time, the second time or even the third time. It got to be accepted." Since mission control had tracked the foam loss during the launch of STS-107, the report noted, NASA could have directed the crew to inspect and try to repair the wing during their fifteen days in orbit. Or they could have launched another shuttle to rescue the crew. Instead, said Sally, "They assumed the foam was not going to be a problem." For that reason, the CAIB reported that, "In the board's view, NASA's organizational culture and structure had as much to do with this accident as the external tank foam."

Based on their investigation, the CAIB made close to thirty short- and long-term recommendations to NASA. They asked that an independent engineering group be established to make sure each shuttle was ready to be launched. They called for the space agency to develop a plan to eliminate the shedding of any debris from the external fuel tank. They required that NASA find ways to inspect and repair any damage to shuttle vehicles early in their missions. To help with these inspections, they insisted that more and better images be taken of the shuttle during each mission. That included requiring orbiting satellites to take images of every shuttle while it was in flight. The board emphasized improving maintenance and safety standards, too. They asked NASA to redesign its data system to include information on the performance and health of the shuttle. They also called for more rigorous training for the mission managers on the ground, including challenges that required lifesaving problem solving.

Close to two years after the CAIB issued its report in August 2003, shuttle launches resumed. On July 26, 2005, seven astronauts lifted off aboard the space shuttle *Discovery* for STS-114, a fifteen-day mission. While training for the trip, the commander, Eileen Collins, talked about the risks involved. "There are risks in spaceflight and there are unknowns," she said. "We try to understand as much of it as we can. . . . We will always remember our friends, but it's time to take what they lived for and what they believed in—space exploration—and move on and get the shuttle flying again." Despite the precautions taken as a result of the CAIB report, debris once again separated from the external fuel tank during the launch of STS-114. Fortunately, this time the debris did not impact the mission. But after the successful completion of STS-114, NASA once again grounded its shuttle fleet. The next shuttle would not lift off until July 4, 2006, after more improvements had been made.

Following her work on the CAIB, Sally returned to her mission of encouraging young people—especially girls—to pursue careers in science. She continued to be the face of Imaginary Lines, so much so that the company adopted a new name, Sally Ride Science. She also joined the public outcry when the president of Harvard University, Lawrence Summers, suggested at a conference that boys may be inherently more gifted in science and math than girls. "I was trying to provoke discussion," said Summers of his remarks on January 14, 2005, and did he ever. Sally was one of eighty male and female leaders in science, engineering, and education who rejected his claim in a letter to *Science* magazine. It stated, "If society, institutions, teachers, and leaders like President Summers expect . . . that girls and women will not perform as well as boys and men, there is a good chance many will indeed not perform as well. . . . We must continue to address the multitude of small and subtle ways in which people of all kinds are discouraged from pursuing interest in scientific and technical fields."

Meanwhile Sally had started to collect honors for her work at NASA and beyond. In 1985 she was inducted into the International Space Hall of Fame at the New Mexico Museum of Space History. Three years later she was inducted into the National Women's Hall of Fame in Seneca Falls, New York. In 2003 Sally was the first woman ever inducted into the US Astronaut Hall of Fame at the Kennedy Space Center in Florida. When fellow astronaut Bob Crippen introduced her at that ceremony, he referred to their 1983 mission, STS-7. "On that flight," he said, "this new inductee broke perhaps the world's highest glass ceiling."

More distinctions followed. In 2005 the National Collegiate Athletics Association (NCAA) honored Sally with the Theodore Roosevelt Award. The "Teddy" is given to a graduate of an NCAA college or university whose experiences as a varsity athlete were a springboard to "a distinguished career of national significance and achievement." Previous winners included US presidents Gerald Ford, Ronald Reagan, George H. W. Bush, and Dwight D. Eisenhower, as well as African-American tennis pioneer Althea Gibson and Eunice Kennedy Shriver, founder of the Special Olympics. In 2006 Sally was one of the first thirteen men and women—also including Billie Jean King and Walt Disney—inducted into the California Hall of Fame in Sacramento. The following year she was inducted into the National Aviation Hall of Fame in Dayton, Ohio. Others in that hall included aviation giants Wilbur and Orville Wright and Amelia Earhart.

As the honors poured in, Sally worked to expand her company's impact. Sally Ride Science began to develop classroom sets of supplemental science materials on topics including climate change and astronomy. They introduced Educator Institutes to give teachers activities and strategies for getting their students excited about science, technology, engineering, and math. They also started producing short, stand-alone What Do You Want to Be? books that introduced young readers to women in a whole host of science careers. At the same time, Sally and Tam continued to write books together. *Mission Planet Earth: Our World and Its Climate—and How Humans Are Changing Them* came out in 2009. So did a companion volume, *Mission Save the Planet: Things You Can Do to Help Fight Global Warming.*

In November 2009 President Barack Obama called upon Sally to play an important role in his Educate to

Innovate campaign, designed to provide students with the skills to succeed in STEM careers. "Scientists and engineers ought to stand side by side with athletes and entertainers as role models," said the president, "and here at the White House, we're going to lead by example. We're going to show young people how cool science can be." The campaign included special science programming on TV and an annual science fair at the White House. It also depended on industry leaders to support STEM education programs. Toward that end, Sally helped to recruit more than one hundred heads of US corporations to launch Change the Equation in September 2010. This nonprofit group aimed to encourage businesses to fund and get involved in STEM programs in their communities. The ultimate goal was to raise the level of learning for all students, giving them the tools they needed to become the future innovators in American industry.

Sally's passion for science education was infectious, and Change the Equation gave her the satisfaction of having powerful partners in the fight for science literacy. But only six months after the organization was founded, Sally received somber news. She had cancer. Sally's cancer originated in the pancreas, a gland in the back of the abdomen.

Part of the digestive system, the pancreas releases enzymes that help break down food in the small intestine. It also releases insulin, a hormone that helps regulate the body's sugar level. Pancreatic cancer develops when abnormal cells grow out of control within the pancreas. Because this type of cancer does not always cause symptoms at its earliest stages, it often is not diagnosed until it is advanced. For that reason, the prognosis is poor. Pancreatic cancer is the fourth most common cause of cancer-related deaths in the United States.

True to form, Sally kept news of her cancer private. During the seventeen months she was ill, she shared the information with officials at NASA but asked them not to publicize it. They complied with her wishes. Sally stopped making public appearances in 2011. She died on July 23, 2012, at the home she shared with Tam O'Shaughnessy in La Jolla, California. She was survived by her partner, Tam; her mother, Joyce; her sister, Bear; a niece; and a nephew. Sally's father, Dale, had died in 1989.

News of Sally's death brought an outpouring of affection from men and women across the country and around the world. In tweets and blogs, in newspaper obituaries and TV spots, people expressed their sadness at Sally's passing and their admiration for the pioneer who showed them that women could break through any barrier, no matter how high. Among the first to mourn her was President Obama. "Sally was a national hero and a powerful role model," he said. "Sally's life showed us that there are no limits to what we can achieve and I have no doubt that her legacy will endure for years to come."

AUTHOR'S NOTE
LEGACY

THERE ARE PROS AND CONS TO WRITING A BIOG-
raphy about someone who lived during your own lifetime.
One of the pros is that you bring an inherent understanding of the context of your subject's life. I was born only
three years after Sally, in somewhat similar circumstances,
so I know what the world was like when she was growing
up. It's also helpful that I witnessed the history that she
was a part of, from her shuttle missions to the devastating
Challenger and *Columbia* accidents. Besides doing research
to understand the country's mood for those events, I can
access my own memories.

One of the cons in writing about a current figure is
that the jury still may be out on her place in history. Without the benefit of time, we might not yet know the true
significance of her life. But I don't think that's the case with

Sally Ride. A generation of young women has grown up since Sally's barrier-breaking shuttle mission in 1983, and many of them drew inspiration from her example. "Sally was a personal and professional role model to me and thousands of women around the world," said Lori Garver, deputy administrator of NASA, after Sally's death. "Her spirit and determination will continue to be an inspiration for women everywhere."

Sally's legacy also lives on through her company, Sally Ride Science, which carries on her drive to "put a female face on math and science" with science festivals, educator workshops, and other innovative programs. It lives on through R/V *Sally Ride*, a research ship operated by the Scripps Institution of Oceanography in La Jolla, California, on behalf of the US Navy. When the ship was named after Sally in April 2013, Secretary of the Navy Ray Mabus said, "I named R/V *Sally Ride* to honor a great researcher, but also to encourage generations of students to continue exploring, discovering, and reaching for the stars."

Students of at least two elementary schools in the United States are reminded of Sally's accomplishments every day. The kids at the Sally K. Ride Elementary School in The Woodlands, Texas, call themselves the

Challengers. Those at the Dr. Sally K. Ride Elementary School in Germantown, Maryland, are the Eagles. Sally's legacy is shared by older students too. In May 2013 NASA announced that as many as ten students per year would be able to take part in the new Sally Ride Internship program. The program allows interns to work on projects side by side with practicing scientists and engineers at NASA research centers across the country.

NASA's Sally Ride Internship program was unveiled during a national tribute to Sally at the JFK Center for the Performing Arts in Washington DC on May 20, 2013. The tribute included speeches by tennis pioneer Billie Jean King and Senator Barbara Mikulski of Maryland. The senator had witnessed the launch of Sally's first shuttle mission in Florida. "The ground was shaking," she remembered, "because Dr. Sally Ride had gone where no woman had gone before. There was no going back. She took all American women with her." Before the tribute was over, NASA's administrator, Charles Bolden, told the audience that President Obama planned to bestow the Presidential Medal of Freedom on Sally. That medal is the nation's highest civilian honor.

Sally's spaceflights made her a symbol of women's

advances in American society, but she didn't measure success based on what others thought about her. "I actually measure it by personal satisfaction," she said in 2006. "The best advice I can give anybody is to try to understand who you are and what you want to do, and don't be afraid to go down that road. Do whatever it takes and work as hard as you have to work to achieve that."

ACKNOWLEDGMENTS

AS SOON AS I GOT THE ASSIGNMENT TO WRITE this book, I called my former colleague Nancy Finton. Nancy spent several years working with Sally Ride at Space.com and Imaginary Lines, and she readily agreed to meet me over lunch to share her memories and impressions. It was a great way to start my research, and I truly appreciate her help.

Next came a bit of kismet. My friend Gary Reisner happened to work with retired astronaut Kathryn Sullivan at the National Oceanic and Atmospheric Administration (NOAA) in Washington DC, and he graciously volunteered to ask her if she would submit to an interview. I thank Gary for reaching out, and I thank Dr. Sullivan for the unforgettable opportunity to learn what astronauts are made of and to hear about her years at NASA with Sally.

Thanks, also, to author Karen Blumenthal for her tremendous generosity in sharing the interview she did with Sally while she was working on her award-winning book, *Let Me Play: The Story of Title IX: The Law That Changed*

ACKNOWLEDGMENTS

the Future of Girls in America. And thanks to Elizabeth Borja and the staff at the library of the Smithsonian National Air and Space Museum in Washington for jump-starting my research on Sally and the history of women in the space program.

Sally Ride started with an e-mail from my editor and longtime friend Karen Nagel. I thank her, Bethany Buck, and everyone else at Aladdin for their confidence in me and their help along the way. I also thank my personal support system, including my parents; my brother, Buddy; and all the friends who were around during the creative process, especially Jackie Glasthal for being a willing and patient sounding board.

This book is dedicated to the memory of Mary Rose Dallal, who continued to live an extraordinary life while fighting her own battle against pancreatic cancer for more than six years.

TIME LINE

May 26, 1951: Sally Kristen Ride is born in Los Angeles, California.

October 4, 1957: The Soviet Union launches the satellite *Sputnik I* into orbit, spurring the United States to try and catch up in the "Space Race."

July 29, 1958: President Dwight D. Eisenhower signs the National Aeronautics and Space Act, creating NASA.

April 12, 1961: Yuri Gagarin of the Soviet Union becomes the first human in space.

May 5, 1961: Alan Shepard becomes the first American in space.

June 16, 1963: Valentina Tereshkova of the Soviet Union becomes the first woman in space.

1968: Sally graduates from the Westlake School for Girls in Los Angeles.

January 3, 1972: NASA's administrator says that both men and women will fly on the space shuttles that the agency plans to build.

1973: Sally graduates from Stanford with a BA in English and a BS in physics.

1975: Sally receives a master's degree in physics from Stanford.

January 16, 1978: NASA announces its new class of thirty-five astronauts, including Sally and five other women.

1978: Sally receives a PhD in physics from Stanford.

TIME LINE

August 19, 1982: Svetlana Savitskaya of the Soviet Union becomes the second woman in space.

June 18–24, 1983: Sally becomes the first American woman in space on STS-7.

October 5–13, 1984: Sally returns to space on STS-41G.

January 28, 1986: The entire crew is lost when the *Challenger* explodes after takeoff.

1987: After serving on the Rogers Commission and publishing her own report on NASA's future, Sally retires from the space agency to teach at Stanford.

1989: Sally becomes a professor of physics and the director of CalSpace at the University of California, San Diego.

2001: With Tam O'Shaughnessy and others, Sally founds Imaginary Lines, Inc.

2003: Sally serves on the panel investigating the loss of the space shuttle *Columbia* and its crew on February 1.

September 2010: Sally helps to create Change the Equation, a nonprofit group that motivates businesses to get involved in STEM programs in their communities.

July 23, 2012: Sally dies of pancreatic cancer.

December 17, 2012: NASA names the lunar landing site of its two GRAIL (Gravity Recovery and Interior Laboratory) satellites after Sally.

November 20, 2013: Tam O'Shaughnessy accepts the Presidential Medal of Freedom from President Obama on Sally's behalf.

FURTHER READING
AND VIEWING

BOOKS BY SALLY RIDE

Ride, Sally, with Susan Okie. *To Space & Back.* New York: Lothrop, Lee & Shepard Books, 1986.

Ride, Sally, and Tam O'Shaughnessy. *Voyager: An Adventure to the Edge of the Solar System.* New York: Crown Books for Young Readers, 1992.

———. *The Third Planet: Exploring Earth from Space.* New York: Crown Books for Young Readers, 1994.

———. *The Mystery of Mars.* New York: Crown Books for Young Readers, 1999.

———. *Exploring Our Solar System.* New York: Crown Books for Young Readers, 2003.

———. *Mission Planet Earth: Our World and Its Climate—and How Humans Are Changing Them.* New York: Roaring Brook Press, 2009.

———. *Mission Save the Planet: Things You Can Do to Help Fight Global Warming.* New York: Roaring Brook Press, 2009.

BOOKS BY OTHERS

Stone, Tanya Lee. *Almost Astronauts: 13 Women Who Dared to Dream.* Somerville, MA: Candlewick Press, 2009.

Weitekamp, Margaret A. *Right Stuff, Wrong Sex: America's First Women in Space Program.* Baltimore: Johns Hopkins University Press, 2004.

FURTHER READING AND VIEWING

ON THE WEB

"The Impact of Sally Ride's Contributions in Space and Education"
youtube.com/watch?v=4T8X1GksQaY
Ninety-minute lecture and panel discussion presented at the Smithsonian National Air and Space Museum on May 17, 2013, to honor the legacy of Sally Ride.

NASA Johnson Space Center Oral History Project
jsc.nasa.gov/history/oral_histories/participants.htm
Access the transcripts of in-depth interviews with scores of astronauts and other NASA personnel from the list found here.

Sally Ride EarthKAM
earthkam.ucsd.edu/home
Sign up to take part in EarthKAM's next mission, or view and download some of the photographs taken in the past.

Sally Ride Science
sallyridescience.com
On the website of the company she founded, learn about Sally and the educational programs she developed.

STS-7 Postflight Video
nss.org/resources/library/shuttlevideos/shuttle07.htm
Astronauts Ride, Crippen, Hauck, Fabian, and Thagard narrate a sixteen-minute video about their 1983 shuttle flight.

STS-41G Flight Video
nss.org/resources/library/shuttlevideos/shuttle13.htm
Sally and the crew narrate a video about their 1984 shuttle mission.

Women@NASA: Women & Girls Initiative
women.nasa.gov
Videos and essays from many of the women who work in science, technology, engineering, and math (STEM) careers at NASA today.

SOURCES

BOOKS

Committee on Human Spaceflight Crew Operations, National Research Council. *Preparing for the High Frontier: The Role and Training of NASA Astronauts in the Post–Space Shuttle Era*. Washington, D.C.: The National Academies Press, 2011.

Danzig, Allison and Peter Schwed. *The Fireside Book of Tennis*. New York: Simon and Schuster, 1972.

Grimsley, Will. *Tennis: Its History, People and Events*. Englewood, N.J.: Prentice-Hall, Inc., 1971.

Ride, Sally with Susan Okie. *To Space & Back*. New York: Lothrop, Lee & Shepard Books, 1986.

Stone, Tanya Lee. *Almost Astronauts: 13 Women Who Dared to Dream*. Somerville, MA: Candlewick Press, 2009.

Weitekamp, Margaret A. *Right Stuff, Wrong Sex: America's First Women in Space Program*. Baltimore: Johns Hopkins University Press, 2004.

ARTICLES AND DOCUMENTS

Adler, Jerry with Pamela Abramson. "Sally Ride: Ready for Liftoff." *Newsweek*, June 13, 1983.

"Astronaut Sally Ride: A Multi-Talented Dynamo." *Alton (IL) Telegraph*, June 14, 1983. clickamericana.com/topics/discoveries-inventions/astronaut-sally-ride-a-multi-talented-dynamo-1983.

Beyette, Beverly. "Wimbledon Puts Alice Back in Wonderland." *Los Angeles Times*, June 22, 1983.

SOURCES

Borgman, Jim. Political Cartoon. *Cincinnati Enquirer*, reprinted in *Newsweek*, June 13, 1983.

Bracken, Nicole M., and Erin Irick. *2004–10 NCAA Gender-Equity Report*. Indianapolis: National Collegiate Athletic Association, November 2011. ncaapublications.com/productdownloads/GEQ2010.pdf.

Broad, William J. "Perfect Landing by Shuttle Marks Return to Florida." *New York Times*, October 14, 1984.

———. "Shuttle Lifts Off for 8-Day Mission with Record Crew." *New York Times*, October 6, 1984.

Bureau of the Census. Fifteenth Census of the United States, 1930. [Listing of Thomas V. Ride]

Bureau of the Census. Sixteenth Census of the United States, 1940. [Listing of Thomas V. Ride]

Chang, Kenneth. "White House Begins Campaign to Promote Science and Math Education." *New York Times*, November 23, 2009.

Columbia Accident Investigation Board. *Report*. Washington, D.C., August 2003. history.nasa.gov/columbia/CAIB_reportindex.html.

Dembart, Lee. "Being Female Is Not Significant, Astronaut Says." *Los Angeles Times*, May 25, 1983.

Dillon, Sam. "Harvard Chief Defends His Talk on Women." *New York Times*, January 18, 2005.

Dunn, Marcia. "Sally Ride, 3 Others Join Astronaut Hall of Fame." *The Lakeland (FL) Ledger*, June 22, 2003.

Foster, Amy. "The Gendered Anniversary: The Story of America's Women Astronauts." *Florida Historical Quarterly*, Vol. 87, No. 2, Fall 2008, pp. 150–173.

SOURCES

"From the Beginning to the End." *New York Times*, January 29, 1986.

Goodman, Ellen. "Sally Ride Bore the Burden of 'First Woman' with Dignity." *Deseret News*, June 25, 1983.

Hendrix, Kathleen. "Astronaut Sally Ride: The Sky May Not Be Her Limit." *Los Angeles Times*, May 13, 1982.

Hughes, Sarah Ann. "Astronaut Sally Ride Honored at Kennedy Center, Will Receive Presidential Medal of Freedom." *DCist Daily*, May 21, 2013. dcist.com/2013/05/late_astronaut_sally_ride_ honored_a.php.

Lamson, David. "Smart Girls Are Helpless." *Saturday Evening Post*, May 26, 1951, pp. 31+.

Lasagna, Louis. "Why Not 'Astronauttes' Also?" *New York Times Magazine*, October 21, 1962.

Lindsey, Robert. "Shuttle Returns, Diverted to Land on the West Coast." *New York Times*, June 25, 1983.

"Loss of the Shuttle: Excerpts from Report of the Columbia Accident Investigation Board." *New York Times*, August 27, 2003.

Muller, Carol B., Sally M. [*sic*] Ride, et al. "Gender Differences and Performance in Science." *Science*, February 18, 2005.

"No White Roses for a Crew Lady." *Washington Post*, June 26, 1983.

Office of the Press Secretary, the White House. "Statement by the President on the Passing of Sally Ride." Washington, D.C., July 23, 2012. whitehouse.gov/the-press-office/2012/07/23/statement-president-passing-sally-ride.

Okie, Susan. "At Home, Space Art and Trivia Tests." *Washington Post*, May 9, 1983.

SOURCES

———. "Cool Hand Sally Showed the Right Stuff." *Washington Post*, May 10, 1983.

———. "Friend Charts Her Path to Space." *Washington Post*, May 8, 1983.

———. "NASA Appeal Gave a Physicist Wings." *Washington Post*, May 9, 1983.

Presidential Commission on the Space Shuttle Challenger Accident. *Report to the President*. Washington, D.C., June 6, 1986. history.nasa.gov/rogersrep/genindex.htm.

———. "My Childhood." *Sally Ride's Blog*, April 30, 2010. mrcsridevg.blogspot.com/2010/04/my-childhood.html.

———. "Single Room, Earth View." *Air & Space*, July 2012. airspacemag.com/space-exploration/Single-Room-Earth-View-163470026.html?c=y&page=1.

———. *Leadership and America's Future in Space: A Report to the Administrator*. Washington, D.C.: National Aeronautics and Space Administration, August 1987. history.nasa.gov/riderep/begin.htm.

"Ride, Sally K(risten)." *Current Biography*, October 1983.

Robbins, Gary. "New Ship Named After Sally Ride." *San Diego Union-Tribune*, April 13, 2013. utsandiego.com/news/2013/Apr/14/tp-new-ship-named-after-sally-ride/.

Ross-Nazzal, Jennifer. "Legacy of the 35 New Guys." *Houston History*, Fall 2008, pp. 64–70.

Ryan, Michael. "A Ride in Space." *People*, June 20, 1983.

"Sally Ride Wins Net Title at Bryn Mawr by 6–1, 6–1." *New York Times*, May 5, 1969.

SOURCES

Sanborn, Sara. "Sally Ride, Astronaut: The World Is Watching." *Ms.*, January 1983.

Shearer, Lloyd. "Does Sally Ride Want to Be Sold?" *Parade*, August 7, 1983.

United States Congress. Equal Employment Opportunity Amendment to the Civil Rights Act of 1964. Approved March 24, 1972. eeoc.gov/ eeoc/history/35th/thelaw/eeo_1972.html.

University of California, San Diego. "UCSD's Sally Ride Receives NCAA's Highest Honor." [Press Release] San Diego, California, December 2, 2004. ucsdnews.ucsd.edu/newsrel/awards/mcride.asp.

Weintrab, Bernard. "The Shuttle Explosion; Reagan Postpones State of Union Speech." *New York Times*, January 29, 1986.

Wilford, John Noble. "Shuttle Rockets to Orbit with 5 Aboard." *New York Times*, June 19, 1983.

"Women@NASA Honors Sally Ride." NASA Women and Girls Initiative. women.nasa.gov/sallyride.

Wright, Lawrence. "Space Cadet." *Texas Monthly*, July 1981.

Zito, Tom. "On the Cape, Riding High for Sally." *Washington Post*, June 18, 1983.

INTERVIEWS

Crippen, Robert. Interview by Rebecca Wright, NASA Johnson Space Center Oral History Project. Houston, Texas, May 26, 2006. jsc.nasa.gov/history/oral_histories/CrippenRL/CrippenRL_5-26-06.pdf.

Collins, Eileen. "Return to Flight: Preflight Interview: Eileen Collins." NASA, February 23, 2005. nasa.gov/vision/space/preparingtravel/ rtf_interview_collins.html.

SOURCES

Ride, Sally. "A Conversation with Sally Ride: Painful Questions from an Ex-Astronaut." By Claudia Dreifus. *New York Times*, August 26, 2003.

———. "Back to School: The Sally Ride Interview." By Mike Drummond. *Inventors Digest*, August/September 2007.

———. "Female Frontiers QuestChat Archive Featuring: Sally Ride." NASA Quest, March 23, 1999. quest.arc.nasa.gov/space/frontiers/chat_archives/ride03-23-99.html.

———. Interview by Karen Blumenthal, August 4, 2003.

———. Interview by Rebecca Wright, NASA Johnson Space Center Oral History Project. San Diego, California, October 22, 2002. jsc.nasa.gov/history/oral_histories/RideSK/RideSK_10-22-02.pdf.

———. Interview by Rebecca Wright, NASA Johnson Space Center Oral History Project. San Antonio, Texas, December 6, 2002. jsc.nasa.gov/history/oral_histories/RideSK/RideSK_12-6-02.pdf.

———. "Interview: Sally Ride, First American Woman in Space." By the Academy of Achievement. Los Angeles, California, June 2, 2006. achievement.org/autodoc/printmember/rid0int-1.

Sullivan, Kathryn. Interview by Jennifer Ross-Nazzal, NASA Johnson Space Center Oral History Project. Columbus, Ohio, May 10, 2007. jsc.nasa.gov/history/oral_histories/SullivanKD/SullivanKD_5-10-07.htm.

———. Interview by Jennifer Ross-Nazzal, NASA Johnson Space Center Oral History Project, Columbus, Ohio, March 12, 2008. jsc.nasa.gov/history/oral_histories/SullivanKD/SullivanKD_3-12-08.htm.

———. Interview by Sue Macy, October 10, 2012.

SOURCE NOTES

Epigraph

"I would like . . . her goals." Academy of Achievement interview.

Introduction

p. 2: "She doesn't offer . . . doesn't always work, either." Adler, *Newsweek*, p. 38.

Chapter 1

p. 3: "Smart Girls Are Helpless," Lamson, *Saturday Evening Post*.

p. 4: "haven't spoken . . . maybe three." *Alton (IL) Telegraph*.

p. 4: "Dale and I . . . refrained." Ryan, *People*, p. 87.

p. 5: Andy Anderson's story: Ibid., p. 87.

p. 6: Thomas V. Ride's story: Fifteenth Census, 1930, and Sixteenth Census, 1940.

p. 6: "When kids played . . . to the boys." Ryan, *People*, p. 87.

p. 6: Play for the Dodgers: Adler, *Newsweek*, p. 45.

p. 6: Fan of James Bond and science fiction: Sanborn, *Ms.*, p. 47.

p. 6: Piano lessons: Adler, *Newsweek*, p. 45.

p. 7: Her father's sabbatical: Some sources say she was ten, but Sally herself says nine in "My Childhood," *Sally Ride's Blog*.

p. 7: Her father quit playing competitive tennis: Hendrix, *Los Angeles Times*, May 13, 1982.

SOURCE NOTES

p. 8: "He said, 'Go out and play' . . . boys." Grimsley, *Tennis: Its History, People and Events*, p. 150.

p. 8: "was the product . . . overheads." Danzig and Schwed, *The Fireside Book of Tennis*, p. 314.

p. 9: "She had talent . . . perfect aim." Beyette, *Los Angeles Times*, June 22, 1983.

p. 9: Missing church: Adler, *Newsweek*, p. 45.

p. 10: "Sally was a fleet-footed . . . instantaneous." Okie, *Washington Post*, May 8, 1983.

p. 10: Without losing a set and cool and self-confident: *Alton (IL) Telegraph*.

p. 11: One hundred miles per hour and "How to handle . . . perspective." Hendrix, *Los Angeles Times*.

Chapter 2

p. 12: "Dr. Mommaerts . . . emotional fulfillment." Okie, *Washington Post*, May 8, 1983.

p. 13: "She was obviously . . . personified before." Adler, *Newsweek*, p. 49.

p. 13: "Math and science . . . sort of thing" and "I was . . . to read it." Blumenthal interview.

p. 14: "gave me a lot . . . science major." Ibid.

p. 14: "She cared . . . of her." Okie, *Washington Post*, May 8, 1983.

p. 14: "I was going to be . . . tennis pro." Blumenthal interview.

p. 15: By comparison, in 2010 alone, Division 1 schools offered women an average of $2 million in sports scholarship money per school. *2004–10 Gender-Equity Report*, p. 19.

p. 15: Physics major: Sanborn, *Ms.*, p. 48.

p. 15: "Miss Ride . . . forceful hitting." *New York Times*, May 5, 1969.

p. 15: "Sally Ride . . . in the East." *Daily Times* quoted in Hendrix, *Los Angeles Times*.

p. 16: "I thought . . . to be doing." Blumenthal interview.

p. 16: "took a long . . . with that forehand." Academy of Achievement interview.

p. 17: "She stopped playing . . . where she wanted." Adler, *Newsweek*, pp. 45, 49.

p. 17: Sally's idol: Blumenthal interview.

p. 17: Urged Sally to become a pro: Adler, *Newsweek*, p. 45.

pp. 17–18: "I wasn't . . . small" and "just loved physics . . . conduct physics research." Blumenthal interview.

p. 19: "Like most science majors . . . Shakespeare." Sanborn, *Ms.*, p. 48.

p. 19: "kind of like doing . . . you were right." *Current Biography*.

pp. 20–21: "The moment I saw . . . that adventure," and "I can still . . . at the time." Academy of Achievement interview.

p. 22: "I didn't think . . . selected." Ibid.

Chapter 3

p. 23: "we had a new . . . backgrounds and ages." "NASA Appeal," Okie, *Washington Post*, May 9, 1983.

p. 24: "based on . . . national origin." Equal Employment Opportunity Amendment to the Civil Rights Act of 1964, Section 717.

p. 24: seventy-three astronauts: *Preparing for the High Frontier*, p. 12.

pp. 24–25: "I knew . . . could do it well." Weitekamp, *Right Stuff, Wrong Sex*, p. 69.

p. 25: "I put in . . . under no circumstances." Ibid., p. 71.

p. 27: "We are already . . . male colleagues." Ibid., p. 77.

p. 27: "They never . . . talk about it." Stone, *Almost Astronauts*, p. 56.

p. 28: "We seek . . . in the past." Ibid., p. 67.

p. 28: "It is inconceivable . . . men only." Ibid., p. 68.

p. 28: George Low on NASA's priorities: Foster, *The Florida Historical Quarterly*, p. 153.

p. 29: "The failure . . . a man's world." Lasagna, *New York Times Magazine*, pp. 60, 62.

p. 30: "No special flight training . . . into space." Foster, *The Florida Historical Quarterly*, p. 156.

p. 31: "I am sure . . . qualified selection." Ibid., p. 157.

p. 31: Numbers of male and female applicants: Stone, *Almost Astronauts*, p. 97.

p. 32: "Nobody knew . . . anything!" Sanborn, *Ms.*, p. 48.

p. 33: "The first guy . . . feel about you?" Ibid., p. 48.

p. 33: "was sort of . . . rattle you." "NASA Appeal," Okie, *Washington Post*, May 9, 1983.

p. 34: "Team players . . . *have* to be team players." Sanborn, *Ms.*, p. 48.

p. 34: "We've got a job . . . taking it." "NASA Appeal," Okie, *Washington Post*, May 9, 1983.

p. 34: "I thought . . . give them the news!" Sally Ride interview by Rebecca Wright, October 22, 2002.

SOURCE NOTES

Chapter 4

p. 37: "I mean, my gosh . . . my day." Ride interview by Wright, October 22, 2002.

p. 38: "We eventually . . . way late." Kathryn Sullivan interview by Jennifer Ross-Nazzal, May 10, 2007.

pp. 38–39: "It was almost . . . to Houston." Ride interview by Wright, October 22, 2002.

p. 39: Only five or six were female: Ibid.

p. 39: Complained no astronaut was present: Okie, *Washington Post*, May 10, 1983.

p. 40: "The selection committee . . . within our group." Ride interview by Wright, October 22, 2002.

p. 40: "Many people . . . as well as males do." Wright, *Texas Monthly*, p. 186.

p. 41: "It was just like . . . trained to do." Ride interview by Wright, October 22, 2002.

p. 43: "The flying . . . flight training itself." Ibid.

p. 44: "Until you . . . to work." Ibid.

Chapter 5

p. 49: "They were both . . . their cameras" and "The crew . . . features on the ground." Ride interview by Wright, October 22, 2002.

p. 50: "I like people . . . with me." Okie, *Washington Post*, May 10, 1983.

pp. 50–51: "I think NASA . . . we had onboard." Robert Crippen interview by Rebecca Wright.

p. 51: "I have to admit . . . about." Okie, *Washington Post*, May 10, 1983.

p. 51: "He reminded . . . space center." Ride interview by Wright, October 22, 2002.

p. 52: "They did a really . . . team thing." Ibid.

p. 52: "Somebody had to . . . being first." Okie, *Washington Post*, May 10, 1983.

p. 53: "We got to . . . the training." Ride interview by Wright, October 22, 2002.

p. 54: "We eat . . . potato chips." "At Home, Space Art and Trivia Tests," Okie, *Washington Post*, May 9, 1983.

p. 55: "I think that's . . . enlightened." Dembart, *Los Angeles Times*.

p. 55: "Why doesn't . . . questions?" Ibid.

p. 56: "I am so excited . . . ignore all you people." Ibid.

p. 56: "Who will make . . . knit?" Borgman, *Cincinnati Enquirer*.

pp. 56–57: "As a First Woman . . . is fine." Goodman, *Deseret News*.

p. 57: "It came with . . . make any mistakes." Blumenthal interview.

Chapter 6

pp. 60–61: "We understand . . . to the country." Zito, *Washington Post*.

p. 62: "Sally . . . Friday." Wilford, *New York Times*.

p. 62: "Have you ever . . . E ticket." Ibid.

p. 63: "At first . . . get into orbit." Ride and Okie, *To Space & Back*, p. 18.

p. 64: "I soon learned . . . anchored in place." Ibid., pp. 30–31.

p. 66: "The act of releasing . . . the satellite?'" Ride interview by Wright, October 22, 2002.

p. 67: "We spent a lot . . . that took it." Ibid.

p. 67: "From space shuttle height . . . nature's phenomena." Ride, *Air & Space*.

SOURCE NOTES

pp. 67–68: "A modern city . . . materializes." Ibid.

p. 71: "just a most thrilling . . . the job." Lindsey, *New York Times*.

p. 71: "She had said . . . crewmates." *Washington Post*, June 26, 1983.

pp. 71–72: "While I was training . . . the flight." Ride interview by Wright, October 22, 2002.

p. 72: "Thank goodness . . . again." Ibid.

Chapter 7

p. 73: "I actually don't . . . the details." Ride interview by Wright, October 22, 2002.

pp. 74–75: "Sally was . . . surrounding her" and "people would come . . . 'NOT SALLY.'" Kathryn Sullivan interview by Jennifer Ross-Nazzal.

p. 76: "Part of my job . . . run a crew." Ride interview by Wright, October 22, 2002.

p. 79: "had very much . . . the first." Ibid.

p. 79: "You really can . . . having fun." Broad, *New York Times*, October 6, 1984.

p. 81: "Under normal circumstances . . . worked quite well." Ride interview by Wright, October 22, 2002.

p. 82: "Before long . . . sneak outside." Sullivan interview by Ross-Nazzal, March 12, 2008.

p. 83: "The third . . . charm." Broad, *New York Times*, October 14, 1984.

p. 84: "There was a fair . . . after STS-7." Ride interview by Wright, October 22, 2002.

Chapter 8

p. 87: "I pulled out . . . Astronaut Office at JSC." Ride interview by Wright, October 22, 2002.

p. 88: "Flight controllers . . . major malfunction." "From the Beginning to the End," *New York Times*.

p. 88: "I know it's hard . . . to follow them." Weintrab, *New York Times*.

p. 90: "I was just going . . . followed the accident." Ride interview by Wright, October 22, 2002.

pp. 90–91: "The panel . . . should be held." Ibid.

p. 91: "The specific failure . . . to this failure." *Report to the President*, "Chapter IV: The Cause of the Accident," p. 40.

pp. 91–92: "The Space Shuttle's . . . flight risk." Ibid., p. 120.

p. 93: "I decided . . . recovery process." Ride interview by Wright, October 22, 2002.

p. 94: Four major projects: Ride, *Leadership and America's Future in Space*.

p. 96: "I'd been doing . . . not looking." Sally Ride interview by Rebecca Wright, December 6, 2002.

p. 97: "A lot of girls . . . through that." Blumenthal interview.

Chapter 9

pp. 98–99: "If a girl . . . math and science." Blumenthal interview.

p. 99: "called me . . . Voyager spacecraft." Ride interview by Wright, December 6, 2002.

pp. 100–101: "We fly . . . center at UCSD." Sally Ride interview on NASA Quest, March 23, 1999.

pp. 101–2: "The vision at the time . . . everyone." Ride interview by Wright, December 6, 2002.

p. 102: "I started thinking . . . Imaginary Lines." Ride interview by Wright, December 6, 2002.

SOURCE NOTES

pp. 102–3: "What drove me . . . gone away." Dreifus interview, *New York Times*.

p. 103: "We wanted a name . . . to women." Blumenthal interview.

p. 103: Sally's 1983 salary: Shearer, *Parade*.

p. 103: "Her exploits . . . the whole works." Ibid.

p. 104: Make a million dollars: Ibid.

p. 104: "I felt . . . worthwhile." Ride interview by Wright, December 6, 2002.

p. 104: "We're doing summer . . . around the country." Blumenthal interview.

pp. 104–5: "We're getting . . . right for this." Ride interview by Wright, December 6, 2002.

p. 105: "Our TOY challenge . . . engineering in disguise." Drummond, *Inventors Digest*, p. 19.

p. 106: "put a female . . . math and science." Ibid., p. 19.

Chapter 10

pp. 109–10: "There are many parallels . . . were seen." Dreifus interview, *New York Times*.

p. 110: "significant . . . foam loss." Columbia Accident Investigation Board, *Report*, Volume 1: Chapter 6, p. 128.

p. 110–11: "There was never . . . to be accepted." Dreifus interview, *New York Times*.

p. 111: "They assumed . . . problem." Ibid.

p. 111: "In the board's view . . . tank foam." "Loss of the Shuttle," *New York Times*, August 27, 2003.

p. 112: "There are risks . . . flying again." Collins interview, February 23, 2005.

p. 113: "I was trying . . . discussion." Dillon, *New York Times*.

p. 113: "If society . . . and technical fields." Muller, Ride, et al., *Science*, p. 1,043.

p. 114: "On that flight . . . glass ceiling." Dunn, *The Lakeland (FL) Ledger*.

p. 114: "a distinguished . . . achievement." "UCSD's Sally Ride Receives NCAA's Highest Honor," December 2, 2004.

p. 116: "Scientists and engineers . . . science can be." Chang, *New York Times*.

p. 118: "Sally was a national hero . . . years to come." "Statement by the President on the Passing of Sally Ride," July 23, 2012.

Author's Note

p. 120: "Sally was a personal . . . for women everywhere." "Women@ NASA Honors Sally Ride."

p. 120: "put a female . . . math and science." Drummond, *Inventors Digest*.

p. 120: "I named . . . for the stars." Robbins, *San Diego Union-Tribune*.

p. 121: "The ground . . . women with her." Hughes, *DCist Daily*.

p. 122: "I actually measure . . . to achieve that." Academy of Achievement interview.

INDEX

INDEX

INDEX

INDEX

INDEX

INDEX

INDEX